TALES OF A POULTRY FARM

Look for these other great books by Clara Dillingham Pierson also from Living Book Press

- Among the Farmyard People
- Among the Pond People
- Among the Forest People
- Among the Meadow People
- Among the Night People
- Dooryard Stories
- Tales from a Poultry Farm

www.livingbookpress.com

This edition published 2021
by Living Book Press

ISBN: 978-1-922634-27-6 (hardcover)
978-1-922634-22-1 (softcover)

First published in 1904.

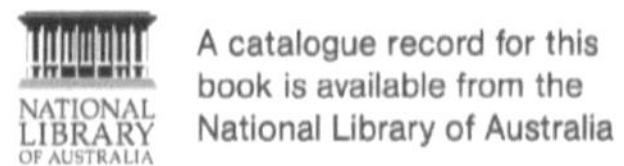

Tales of a Poultry Farm

BY

CLARA DILLINGHAM PIERSON

THEY REACHED QUITE A HIGH BRANCH IN THE APPLE TREE.

CONTENTS

INTRODUCTION

My Dear Little Readers:—I have often wondered why there were not more stories written about Chickens and their friends, and now I am glad that there have been so few, for I have greatly enjoyed writing some for you. Did I ever tell you that I cared for my father's Chickens when I was a little girl? That was one of my duties, and the most pleasant of all. It was not until I was older that I became acquainted with Ducks, Geese, and Turkeys, and I always wish that I might have lived on a poultry farm like the one of which I have written, for then I could have learned much more than I did.

You must not think that I understand no language but English. I learned Chicken-talk when I was very young; and in the fall, when the Quails wander through the stubble-fields near my home, I have many visits with them, calling back and forth "Bob White! Bob White!" and other agreeable things which they like to hear. My little boys can talk exactly like Chickens, and sometimes they pretend that they are Chickens, while I talk Turkey to them.

When you have a chance, you must learn these languages. They are often very useful to one. My friend, who drives in his Hens by imitating the warning cry of a Cock, had been a teacher in a college for several years before he studied poultry-talk, and it helped him greatly.

You see, one must learn much outside of school, as well as inside, in order to be truly well educated. You should never look at poultry and say, "Why, they are only Hens!" or "Why, they are only Ducks!" Quite likely when they look at you they may be thinking, "Why, they are only boys!" or "Why, they are only girls!" Yet if you are gentle and care for them, you and they will learn to think a great deal of each other, and you will win new friends among the feathered people.

Your friend,

CLARA D. PIERSON.

STANTON, MICHIGAN, *March 21, 1904.*

THE FARM IS SOLD

"You stupid creature!" cackled the Brown Hen, as she scrambled out of the driveway. "Don't you know any better than to come blundering along when a body is in the middle of a fine dust bath? How would you like to have me come trotting down the road, just as you were nicely sprawled out in it with your feathers full of dust? I think you would squawk too!"

The Brown Hen drew her right foot up under her ruffled plumage and turned her head to one side, looking severely at Bobs and Snip as they backed the lumber wagon up to the side porch. "I say," she repeated, "that you would squawk too!"

The Brown Hen's friends had been forced to run away when she did, but they had already found another warm place in the dust and were rolling and fluttering happily there. "Come over here," they called to her. "This is just as good a place as the other. Come over and wallow here."

"No!" answered the Brown Hen, putting down her right foot and drawing up her left. "No! My bath is spoiled for to-day. There is no use in trying to take comfort when you are likely to be run over any minute." She turned her head to the other side and looked severely at Bobs and Snip with that eye. The Brown Hen prided herself on her way of looking sternly at people who displeased her. She always wished, however, that she could look at them with both eyes at once. She thought that if this were possible she could stop their nonsense more quickly.

Snip could not say anything just then. He was trying to be polite, and it took all his strength. He was young and wanted to have a good Horse laugh. He could not help thinking how a Horse would look covered with feathers and sprawling in the middle of the road. Of course the Brown Hen had not meant it in exactly that way, but was as unlucky as most people are when they lose their tempers, and amused the very people whom she most wanted to scold.

Bobs was a steady old gray Horse, and he was used to the Brown Hen. "I am sorry that we had to disturb you," he said pleasantly. "You looked very comfortable and I tried to turn out, but the Farmer held the lines so tightly that I could not. The bit cut into my mouth until I could not stand it. You see he wanted to back the wagon up right here, and so he couldn't let us turn out. We'll do better next time if we can."

The Brown Hen let both her feet down and took a few steps forward. "If you couldn't help it, of course I won't say anything more," she remarked, and walked off.

"P-p-p-p-p-p-p-p!" said Snip, blowing the air out between his lips. "Why did you bother to tell her that? She is so fussy and cross about everything that I wouldn't tell her I was sorry. Why doesn't she just find another place, as the other Hens do?"

"Snip," said Bobs, "I used to talk in that way when I was

a Colt, but I find that it makes things a good deal pleasanter around the place if I take a little trouble to say 'I am sorry' when I have to disturb people. You know how the Farmer does at noon? He comes into the stall when I have finished my dinner, and he gives me a pat and says, 'Come along, old fellow. We'd rather be lazy, but we have to work.' Do you think I'd hang back then? I tell you when I want to balk. It is when the Hired Man leads me out with a jerk. That makes me kick."

"I wonder if she will take her dust bath now?" said Snip.

"Oh no," answered Bobs. "Any other Hen on the farm would, but the Brown Hen will not. She will stalk around all day thinking what a hard time she has and talking about it, but she won't take her dust bath, not although every other fowl on the place should wallow beside her."

"Then I don't see what good it did for you to tell her you were sorry," said Snip, who never liked to confess that he was wrong.

"It did a lot of good," said Bobs, steadily. "Before that she was fussy and cross. Now she is only fussy. Besides, I really had to say something to her, and if it had not been pleasant it would have had to be unpleasant, and then there would have been two cross people instead of one. Quite likely there would have been even more before the day was over, for if each of us had gone on being cross we would have made more of our friends cross, and there is no telling where it would have ended. I'd feel mean, anyhow, if I lost my temper with a Hen. Imagine a great big fellow like me getting cross with a little creature like her, who has only two legs, and can't get any water into her stomach without tipping her head back for each billful."

Snip had wanted to ask many more questions, but so much began to happen that he quite forgot about the Brown Hen. The Farmer and the Hired Man had gone into the house, and now they came out, carrying a cook-stove between them. This they put into the wagon, covering it with rag carpet. The Farmer's Wife came to the door with rolled-up sleeves and a towel tied over her head. She looked tired but happy. In her hands she carried the legs of the stove, which she tucked into the oven.

This was a great event to happen on the quiet farm. Brown Bess and her new Calf came close to the fence which separated their pasture from the driveway, and stood looking on. The Pigs and their mother pressed hard against the walls of their pen on the two sides from which anything could be seen. Each of the nine Pigs thought that he had the poorest place for peeping, so he wriggled and pushed and pushed and wriggled to get a better one, and it ended in none of them seeing anything, because they were not still long enough. Their mother, being so much taller than they, had a crack all to herself and could see very well. "I don't understand why they want to do that," she sighed, as she lay down for another nap. "It was after the snow came that they brought the stove out here. But you can never tell what the people who live in houses and wear clothing will do next! They really seem to like to pick things up and carry them around. They are so silly."

The Gander came along with his wife and the other Geese. He ate grass while they visited with the Hens in the road. The Hens told him all they knew, even what the Barred Plymouth Rock Hen had seen when she walked along the porch and peeped in at the open kitchen door. Then the Geese waddled back to where the Gander was and told him all the Hens had told them. He listened to it, asking a good many questions, and then said that it was just like Geese to be so interested in other people's business. That made them feel quite ashamed, so they ate a little grass to make themselves feel better, and then stood around to watch the loading of the wagon.

Besides the stove, the kitchen and dining-room furniture was put in, with a few of the largest plants from the sitting-room, and when the Farmer drove off he had the clock beside him on the seat, the churn between his knees, and a big bundle of some sort on his lap.

It suddenly seemed very dull on the farm. One of the Doves flew along above the team for a while and brought back the news that they had turned toward town. There was nothing now to be done but to wait until they returned and then ask as many questions as possible of the Horses.

"I believe that the family is going to move into town," said the White Cock, who always expected sad things to happen. Even when there was not a cloud in the sky, he was sure that it would rain the next day. That was probably because he was careless about what he ate. The Shanghai Cock said that he did not take half gravel enough, and any sensible fowl will tell you that he cannot be truly happy unless he eats enough gravel.

"What will ever become of us," asked the Hens, "if the family moves to town? It is their business to stay here and take care of us."

"Cock-a-doodle-doo!" crowed the Young Cock. "Let

them go. I can have a good enough time in the fields finding my own food."

The Pullets looked at him admiringly. "But who will take care of us?" they asked.

"I will," said he, holding his head very high. And that was exactly what they wanted him to say, although each of them would rather have had him say it to her alone.

"There will be nobody left to set traps for the Rats and the Weasels," said an old Hen, who had seen much of the ways of poultry-yards. "And if our Chickens have the gapes, who will make horse-hair loops and pull the little Worms out of their throats? I have always said that it was well to have people living in the farmhouse."

"Well," said the Brown Hen, "I hope that if they go they will take the Horses with them. There is no pleasure in life when one is all the time afraid of being run over. You know what happened this morning, when I had started to take my dust bath. I spoke to the Horses about it afterward, and Bobs was very polite, but that didn't give me the bath which he and that silly young Snip had spoiled. And I do not feel at all like myself without a bath."

"Take it now then," said the Shanghai Cock, who never bothered to be polite. "You ought to be able to get it in while the team is going to town and back."

"No," said the Brown Hen, firmly, "it is too far past the time when I should have taken it. I was never one of those Hens who can wallow from morning until night. I need my bath and I ought to have it, but when I have been kept from it so long I simply have to go without it."

The other Hens said nothing. In nearly every poultry-yard there is one fowl who is so fussy as to make everybody else uncomfortable. The rest become used to it after a while and do not answer back when she talks so.

In the house, the Farmer's Wife was hurrying to and fro, showing the Hired Man where to put this or calling him to lift that, and every little while something else would be brought out and placed on the side porch. Once a basket of wax fruit was set on a table there. The glass which usually covered it was put to one side, and the Young Cock who had promised to care for the Pullets flew up to peck at it. He knew it was not right, but he got one hurried billful from the side of the reddest peach just as the Hired Man threw an old shoe at him.

"How does it taste?" cried the Geese, who were still hanging around to find out what they could. The Young Cock did not reply, but wiped his bill on the grass for a long time. He feared he would never be able to open it again. The peaches which he had eaten the fall before had not stuck his bill together in this way, and he was now more sure than ever that the people who lived in houses did not know very much. "Such fruit should be thrown away," he said. "It must be eating such peaches as this which keeps the Boy chewing so much of the time. I have watched him, and he carries something in his mouth which he chews and chews and chews, but never swallows. Once his mother made him throw it away, and I should think she would. He waggled his jaws very much like a Cow." Then he strolled off toward the woods to get away from the other fowls.

In the middle of the afternoon the team came back drawing the empty wagon. All the poultry came sauntering toward the barn, making excuses as they came. "Too hot out in the sunshine," said the Brown Hen. "I really cannot stand it any longer."

"The Geese would come up to the barn," said the Gander, "so I thought I might as well come along."

"Shouldn't wonder if they would throw out some corn when they get through unharnessing," said the Gobbler.

The Ducks never kept up with the others, and they were close to the house when Bobs and Snip stopped there. "How very lucky!" they quacked, for they were a truthful family and not given to making excuses. "We hope you will tell us what all this means. Are the Farmer's people moving away?"

"They are," replied Bobs, who was always good about giving a direct answer to a direct question. "You know the children have been staying in town to go to school ever since last fall, and now their father has sold the farm and is moving into town to be with them."

"Will they take us into town?" asked the Drake.

"Guess not," said Snip. "They are to live over a store."

By this time the disappointed ones who had been waiting in the barn came hurrying along toward the house, where the wagon was being filled once more. It did not take long for the Ducks to tell the news, and then there was great excitement, very great indeed. Brown Bess heard it and licked her Calf more tenderly than ever. She knew that they could not live over a store, and she wondered what would become of them both.

In the Pig-pen the little Pigs were teasing their mother to tell who would bring them their food. It was enough to make her lose her patience to have nine children all asking questions at the same time, and each saying "Why?" every time that he was given an answer. So it is not to be wondered at that she finally became cross and lay down in the corner with her back to them, pretending to be asleep. To tell the truth, she herself was somewhat worried. She had often called the Farmer's family silly, but she had not minded their habit of carrying things around, when the things that they carried were pails full of delicious food and they were carrying them to the Pig-pen.

It was the poultry who talked the longest about the change, and perhaps this was partly because there were so many of them to talk. Poultry have a very happy time on small farms like this one. It is true that they did not have a good house of their own, and they had but little attention paid to them, yet when the cold winter was once past, there was all the lovely spring, summer, and fall weather in which to be happy. They were not kept in a yard, going wherever they chose, finding plenty to eat, and having no cares, excepting that when a Hen felt like it she laid an egg. She laid it wherever she chose, too, and this was usually somewhere in the barn or woodshed. Sometimes Hens wanted to sit, and then they came off after a while with broods of Chickens. When a Hen had done that, she was usually caught and put under a coop for a few days. She never liked that part of it, and the others always told her that if she would hatch out Chickens she might know what to expect.

The winters were bad, but then the poultry spent their whole time in trying to be comfortable and hardly ever bothered to lay eggs, so it was an easy life after all. No wonder that they talked about the change until after they went to roost. Although the Farmer was not a thrifty man, he had been kind enough to the creatures on the farm, and they did not want to go away or belong to any one else.

The last word spoken was by a black Hen. She was not Black Spanish or black anything-in-particular. In fact, there was only one of the Hens who knew to what breed she belonged. That was the Barred Plymouth Rock Hen, and it made her very proud. The Black Hen had a temper, and had even been known to peck at the Farmer's Wife. "Do you know what I will do if a new Farmer tries to make me lay my eggs where he wishes?" she said. "I may have to lay the eggs there, but I will smash every one of them if I do."

THE NEW OWNER COMES

On the morning after the family left, a pale and quiet Man, wearing glasses, came out in a platform wagon to look over the farm. He had been there but a short time when two great loads of furniture appeared down the road. Then the Man took off his coat and helped the drivers carry it all into the little farmhouse. The fowls, who happened to be near enough, noticed that the Man never lifted anything which seemed to be heavy. They noticed, too, that his hands were rather small and very white. Still he acted as though he expected to live on the place. With the others helping him, he put down two carpets and set up two stoves.

The other Men drove away, leaving the single Horse and the platform wagon. The Man washed his hands, put on his coat, and brought a pasteboard box out onto the side porch. He opened it carefully, took out a glass, and drew up a bucketful of water at the well. He filled his glass and carried it back to the porch. Then he began to eat his dinner.

All the farm people had been properly cared for that morning by the Farmer from across the road, and felt sure that he would not see them wanting food, so it was not just a wish for something to eat which made every creature there come quietly to a place near the side porch. They were certain that they belonged to this Man, and they wanted to find out what he was like.

"I hope he isn't expecting to milk me," said Brown Bess. "I don't believe he could draw a drop from my udders, and he would probably set the stool down on the wrong side anyhow."

Bobs and Snip were no longer on the farm, having gone to town, to work there with their old master, so the Hog was the next to speak. "I hope he won't eat that kind of dinner every day," said she. "It looks to me as though there would be no scraps left to go into my pail."

"Ugh! Ugh! Stingy!" grunted the little Pigs. "He wants it all for himself!" They did not stop to think that every time food was emptied into their trough, each of them acted as though he wanted every drop and crumb of it for himself.

The Gobbler strutted up and down near the porch, with his feathers on end and his wings dragging. "There is just one thing I like about the Man," said he. "He does *not* wear a red tie."

"I can't tell exactly what is the matter," said the Gander, "but he is certainly very different from any Man I ever saw before. I think he must belong to a different breed. The things he has on his feet are much blacker and shinier than the Men around here wear, and that stiff and shiny white thing around his neck is much higher. I hope he is not stupid. I cannot bear stupid people."

"Neither can we," murmured the Geese. "We really cannot bear them."

"I fear he does not know very much," said the Drake,

sadly, "although I must say that I like his face. He looks good and kind, not at all as though he would ever throw stones at people for the fun of seeing them waddle faster. What I do not like is the way in which he acted about getting his water. Any Duck knows that you can tell most about people by the way they take water. The old gourd which the Farmer and his family used so long, hung right on the chain-pump, and yet this Man got a glass and filled it. He did not even drink from it as soon as it was full, but filled and emptied it three times before drinking. That is not what I call good sense."

"Did you notice how he put on his coat before he began to eat?" asked the White Cock. "I never saw our Farmer do that except in very cold weather, and I have been close to the kitchen door a great many times when they sat down to the table."

"It must be that he was not very hungry," said one of the Hens, "or he would never have taken so much time to begin eating. Besides, you can see that he was not, by the size of his mouthfuls. He did not take a single bite as big as he could, and you will never make me believe that a person is hungry when he eats in that way." This was the Hen who usually got the largest piece from the food-pan and swallowed it whole to make sure of it, before any of the other fowls could overtake her and get it away.

Then the Barred Plymouth Rock Hen spoke. "I like him," she said. "I am sure that he belongs to a different breed, but I think it is a good one. I remember hearing somebody say, when I was a Chicken, that it was well for fowls to have a change of ground once in a while, and that it would make them stronger. I believe that is why he is here. You can tell by watching him work that he is not strong, and he may be here for a change of ground. I shall certainly befriend him, whatever the rest of you do. We people of fine families should stand by each other." Then she strolled over toward the Man, lifting her feet in her most aristocratic way and perking her head prettily.

The Man smiled. He broke a piece from the slice of bread which he was eating, and sprinkled it lightly with salt from a tiny bottle. This piece he divided into two portions and held one out at arm's length toward the Barred Plymouth Rock Hen. She had never before been invited to eat from anybody's hand, and she was really afraid to do it. Her skin felt creepy, as though her feathers were about to stand on end. Still, she had just said that she meant to befriend the new Man, and that he and she were of finer breeds than most people. Here was her chance to prove her words, and she was not the sort of Hen to show the white feather.

She stood erect in all her Plymouth Rock dignity, and ate the bread in five pecks. Then she stooped and wiped her bill daintily on the grass at the Man's feet before strolling away again.

You can imagine what excitement this made among the poultry. The Gobbler, the Gander, and the Drake did not wish to appear too much interested, and some of the Cocks acted in the same way, but the mothers and sisters of the families talked of nothing else for a long time. It is true that the Barred Plymouth Rock Hen had not been very popular on the farm, most of the Hens insisting that she put on airs, but now they could not help admiring her courage and grace.

Two or three of them even thought she might be right in saying that it was a good thing to come from a fine family. The Cocks had never thought her airy. They always told the other Hens that it was just their notion, and that she was really a very clever and friendly Hen.

As for the Man, he seemed much pleased by what had happened. He put his hat on the back of his head and smiled. "That is a good beginning," he said to himself. "To eat bread and salt together means that we will always be friends, and I would rather break bread with respectable poultry than with some Men that I know."

Late in the afternoon, the Man harnessed his Horse, whom he called Brownie, to the same platform wagon in which he had come, gave one parting look all around the house and yard, turned the key in the side door, and drove off toward town. "What next?" asked all the poultry.

If you had ever been a Hen or a Duck or a Turkey or a Goose (for although you may have acted like a perfect Goose, you probably never have been one), you would know just how worried the poultry on this particular farm were, after the new Man had driven away in the platform wagon. It seemed quite certain that he had gone to town to bring out his family, and it mattered a great deal to them what his family were like. A single Boy of the wrong kind could make all the fowls on the place unhappy, and the others agreed with the Gobbler when he said, "There is one thing worse than a Girl in a red dress, and that is a Boy who throws stones."

It was a very sad company which wandered around the farmyard, picking here and there, and really eating but little.

The White Cock would keep talking about the dreadful things which might happen, and reminded his friends that there might be two Boys, or three, or four, perhaps even five in the family! The other fowls soon tried to get away from him, and then they were often so unfortunate as to meet the Brown Hen, who was fussing and worrying for fear the Man would shut her up in a small yard.

At last the Shanghai Cock lost his temper, as he was very apt to do, and said that there were some fowls he would like to have shut up. This displeased both the White Cock and the Brown Hen, because the Shanghai Cock had looked at both of them when he spoke, using one eye for each, and they did not know what to say. They thought from the mean little cackling laugh which the others gave, that he might have wished them to shut up their bills. Then they did the very best thing that they could have done, going off together to the pasture, where each could talk gloomily to the other without annoying anybody else.

When Brownie came jogging back to the farm, the platform wagon looked very gay. On the back seat sat a pleasant looking Woman with a fat Baby on her lap. Beside her sat a Little Girl with brown hair. On the seat beside the Man sat another Little Girl, dressed exactly like the first one and just as large as she, but with golden hair. They were all laughing and talking and pointing at different things as they drove into the yard.

"It is not much like our other home," said the Man, as he set the Baby on his feet beside the steps, and turned to help the Woman out.

"That does not matter if we can be comfortable and well

here," she answered with a smile. "It will be a lovely place for the children, and I believe it will make you strong again."

"Cock-a-doodle-doo!" said the young Cock from the top rail of the fence. He did it only to show off, but the children, who had never lived on a farm, and so could not understand poultry-talk very well, felt sure that he said, "How-do-you-all-do?" and thought him exceedingly polite. The Baby started after him at once, and fell flat before he had taken six steps.

The Man, the Woman, and the two Little Girls all started to pick up the Baby, who was so wound up in his long cloak that he could not rise. Brownie looked around in a friendly way and stood perfectly still, instead of edging off toward the barn as some Horses would have done, while the Baby just rolled over on his back and laughed.

"Gobble-gobble-gobble!" said the Gobbler. "I think this family will suit us very well."

The Barred Plymouth Rock Hen was too polite a fowl ever to say "I told you so," but she stood very straight and chuckled softly to herself, so the rest could know that she was pleased with what she saw, and felt more certain than ever that the Man and his family were no common people.

All the family went to the barn with the Man while he unharnessed Brownie and gave him his supper. The children had a happy time on the hay, and, before they went into the house together, the Man put some corn in a pan and let them scatter it by the door for the poultry. "They have been running loose in the fields," he said, "and they may not need it all, but we will give it to them anyway, and to-morrow I will study my book of directions and see how they should be fed at this season."

"COCK-A-DOODLE-DOO!" SAID THE YOUNG COCK.

The children scattered the corn, the Woman kneeling down with her arm around the Baby, to keep him from falling over each time that he threw a few kernels. The Barred Plymouth Rock Hen was the first to come forward to pick it up, and the Man told his wife how he and she had eaten bread and salt at noon.

Then the Woman said: "Come, we must go into the house! I should have been there working long ago, but I wanted to see the children make friends with the poultry."

As the door of the house closed behind its new inmates, the Barred Plymouth Rock Hen could not help looking at the Shanghai Cock. "Yes," he said, for he knew what she meant, "I like your friends very much. They seem to have some sense." Then the Barred Plymouth Rock Hen was satisfied, for she was fond of the Shanghai Cock, and praise from him was praise indeed.

THE FIRST SPRING CHICKENS ARE HATCHED

IT was only a few days after the new family settled in the house that the Man drove out from town with a queer-looking box-like thing in his light wagon. This he took out and left on the ground beside the cellarway. When he had unharnessed Brownie and let him loose in the pasture, he came back and took the crate off from the box. Then the poultry who were standing around saw that it was not at all an ordinary box. Indeed, as soon as the Man had fastened a leg to each corner, they thought it rather more like a fat table than a box.

While the Man was examining it, he kept turning over the pages of a small book which he took from some place inside the table. The Geese thought it quite a senseless habit of the Man's, this looking at books when he was at work. They had never seen the Farmer do so, and they did not understand it. When Geese do not understand anything, you know, they always decide that it is very silly and senseless. There are a great many things which they do not understand, so, of course, there are a great many which they think extremely silly.

The Little Girls and their mother stood beside the Man as he looked at the book and the fat new table. He said something to one of them and she went into the house. When she came out she had a small basketful of eggs. The Man took some and put them into one part of the table. Then he took them out again and put them into the basket. That disgusted the Brown Hen, who was watching it all.

"I am always fair," she said, "and I am willing to say that I have been treated very well by this Man, very well indeed, but it is most distressing and unpleasant to a sensible fowl like myself to have to see so much utter foolishness on a farm where I have spent my life."

"Then why don't you shut your eyes?" asked the Shanghai Cock, with his usual rudeness, and after that the Brown Hen could say nothing more. This was a great relief to the Barred Plymouth Rock Hen, who did not at all understand what was going on, but would have tried to defend the Man if the Brown Hen had asked her about it.

After a while the Woman helped the Man carry the queer-looking object into the cellar, and then the poultry strolled off to talk it all over. They heard nothing more about the fat table until the next morning. Then the Gander, who had been standing for a long time close to the cellarway, waddled off toward the barn with the news. "They use that table to keep eggs in," said he. "Now isn't that just like the Man? I saw him put in a great many eggs, and he took them all out of little cases which he brought from town this morning. I don't see why a Man should bring eggs out from town, when he can get plenty in the barn by hunting for them. Do you?"

"He won't find any of mine in the barn," said a Hen Turkey. "I lay one every day, but I never put them there." When she had finished speaking, she looked around to see if the Gobbler had heard her. Luckily he had not. If he had, he would have tried to find and break her eggs.

"That was not the only silly thing the Man did," said the Gander, who intended to tell every bit of news he had, in spite of interruptions.

"Probably not," said the White Cock, who was feeling badly that morning, and so thought the world was all wrong.

"No indeed," said the Gander, raising his voice somewhat, so that the poultry around might know he had news of importance to tell. "No indeed! The Man marked every egg with a sort of stick, which he took from his pocket. It was sharp at both ends, and sometimes he marked with one end and sometimes with the other. He put a black mark on one side of each egg and a red mark on the other."

"Red!" exclaimed the Gobbler. "Ugh!"

"Yes, red," said the Gander. "But the worst and most stupid part of it all was when he lighted a little fire in something that he had and fastened it onto the table."

"What a shame!" cried all the Geese together. "It will burn up those eggs, and every fowl knows that it takes time to get a good lot of them together. He may not have thought of that. He cannot know very much, for he probably never lived on a farm before. He may think that eggs are to be found in barns exactly as stones are found in fields."

All this made the Barred Plymouth Rock Hen very sad. She could not help believing what she had heard, and still she hoped they might yet find out that the Man had a good reason for marking and then burning up those eggs. She was glad to think that none of hers were in the lot. She was not saving them for Chickens just then, but she preferred to think of them as being eaten by the Little Girls or the fat Baby who lived in the house. She decided to begin saving for a brood of Chickens at once. She wanted to say something kind about the Man, or explain what he was doing when he lighted that fire. However, she could not, so she just kept her bill tightly shut and said nothing at all. This also showed that she was a fine Hen, for the best people would rather say nothing at all about others than to say unkind things.

It was a long time before the friendly Barred Plymouth Rock Hen knew what was going on in the cellar. She was greatly discouraged about the Man. She had tried as hard as she could to make the other poultry believe in him, and had thought she was succeeding, but now this foolishness about the fat table and the eggs seemed likely to spoil it all. She found a good place for laying, in a corner of the carriage house on some old bags, and there she put all her eggs. She had decided to raise a brood of Chickens and take comfort with them, leaving the Man to look out for himself as well as he could. She still believed in him, but she was discouraged.

Several of the other Hens also stole nests and began filling them, so on the day when the Man hunted very thoroughly for eggs and found these stolen nests, taking all but one egg from each, there were five exceedingly sad Hens. You would think they might have been discouraged, yet they were not. A Hen may become discouraged about anything else in the world, but if she wants to sit, she sticks to it.

That very day was an exciting one in the cellar. When the Man came down after breakfast to look at the eggs in the fat table he found them all as he had left them, with the black-marked side uppermost. He took them out to air for a few minutes, and then began putting them back with the red-marked side uppermost. As he lifted them, he often put one to his ear, or held it up to the light. He had handled the eggs over in this way twice a day for about three weeks. A few of them had small breaks in the shell, and through one of these breaks there stuck out the tiny beak of an unhatched Chicken. When he found an egg that was cracked, or one in which there seemed to be a faint tap-tap-tapping, he put it apart from the others.

When this was done, the Man ran up the inside stairs. In a few minutes he returned with the Baby in his arms and the rest of the family following. The Woman had her sleeves rolled up and flour on her apron. The Little Girls were dressed in the plain blue denim frocks which they wore all the time, except when they went to town. Then all five of them watched the cracked eggs, and saw the tiny Chickens who were inside chip away the shell and get ready to come out into the great world. The Woman had to leave first, for there came a hissing, bubbling sound from the kitchen above, which made her turn and run up-stairs as fast as she could.

Then what a time the Man had! The Baby in his arms kept jumping and reaching for the struggling Chickens, and the two Little Girls could hardly keep their hands away from them. "Let me help just one get out of his shell," said

RETURNED WITH THE BABY IN HIS ARMS.

the brown-haired Little Girl. "It is *so* hard for such small Chickens."

"No," said the Man, and he said it very patiently, although they had already been begging like this for some time. "No, you must not touch one of them. If you were Hens, you would know better than to want to do such a thing. If you should take the shell off for a Chicken, he would either die or be a very weak little fellow. Before long each will have a fine round doorway at the large end of his shell, through which he can slip out easily."

Some of the Chickens worked faster than others, and some had thin shells to break, while others had quite thick ones, so when the first Chicken was safely out many had not even poked their bills through. As soon as the first was safely hatched, the Man took away the broken shell and closed the fat table again. Then he waved his hat at the Little Girls and said "Shoo! Shoo!" until they laughed and ran out-of-doors.

All that day there were tiny Chickens busy in the incubator (that was what the Man called the fat table), working and working and working to get out of their shells. Each was curled up in a tight bunch inside, and one would almost think that he could not work in such a position. However, each had his head curled around under his left wing, and pecked with it there. Then, too, as he worked, each pushed with his feet against the shell, and so turned very slowly around and around inside it. That gave him a chance, you see, to peck in a circle and so break open a round doorway. As they came out, the Chickens nestled close to each other or ran around a bit and got acquainted, talking in soft little "Cheep-cheep-cheeps."

They were very happy Chickens, for they were warm and had just about light enough for eyes that had seen no light at all until that day. It is true that they had no food, but one does not need food when first hatched, so it is not strange that they were happy. It is also true that they had no mother, yet even that did not trouble them, for they knew nothing at all about mothers. Probably they thought that Chickens were always hatched in incubators and kept warm by lamps.

The next morning, when the Barred Plymouth Rock Hen was sitting on her one egg in the carriage house, thinking sadly of her friend, the Man, that same Man came slowly up to her. The Little Girls were following him, and when they reached the doorway they stood still with their toes on a mark which the Man had made. They wanted very much to see what he was about to do, yet they minded, and stood where they had been told, although they did bend forward as far as they could without tumbling over.

The Man knelt in front of the sitting Hen, and gently uncovered the basket he held. The Hen could hardly believe her ears, for she heard the soft "cheep-cheep-cheep" of newly hatched Chickens. She tried to see into the basket. "There! There!" said the Man, "I have brought you some children." Then he lifted one at a time and slipped it into her nest, until she had twelve beautiful downy white Chickens there.

"Well! Well! Well!" clucked the Hen. And she could not think of another thing to say until the Man had gone off to the barn. He had taken her egg, but she did not care about that. All she wanted was those beautiful Chickens. She fluffed up her feathers and spread out her wings until she covered the whole twelve, and then she was the happiest fowl on the place. The Man came back to put food and water where she could reach both without leaving her nest, and even then she could think of nothing to say.

After he went away, a friend came strolling through the open doorway. This Hen was also sitting, but had come off the nest to stretch her legs and find food. It was a warm April day, and she felt so certain that the eggs would not chill, that she paused to chat.

"Such dreadful luck!" she cackled. "You must never try to make me think that this Man is friendly. He has left me only one of the eggs I had laid, and now I have to start all over for a brood of Chickens, or else give up. The worst of it is that I feel as though I could not lay any more for a while."

"Don't be discouraged," said the Barred Plymouth Rock Hen. "I had only one egg to sit on last night, and this morning I have a whole brood of Chickens."

"Where did they come from?" asked the visiting Hen, in great excitement.

"That is what I don't know," replied the happy mother. "The Man brought them to me just now, and put food and water beside my nest. I have asked and asked them who their mother was, and they say I am the first Hen they ever saw. Of course that cannot be so, for Chickens are not blind at first, like Kittens, but it is very strange that they cannot remember about the Hen who hatched them. They say that there were many more Chickens where they came from, but no Hen whatever."

The White Cock stood in the doorway. "Do you know where my Chickens were hatched?" asked the Barred Plymouth Rock Hen.

"Do I know?" said he, pausing to loosen some mud from one of his feet (he did not understand the feelings of a mother, or he would have answered at once). "I saw the Man bring a basketful of Chickens over this way a while ago. He got them from the cellar. The door was open and I stood on it. Of course I was not hanging around to find out what he was doing. I simply happened to be there, you understand."

"Yes, we understand all about it," said the Hens, who knew the White Cock as well as anybody.

"I happened to be there," he repeated, "and I saw the Man take the Chickens out of the fat table. There was no Hen in sight. It must be a machine for hatching Chickens. I think it is dreadful if the Chickens on this farm have to be hatched in a cellar, without Hens. Everything is going wrong since the Farmer left."

The Barred Plymouth Rock Hen and her caller looked at each other without speaking. They remembered hearing the White Cock talk in that way before the Farmer left. He was one of those fowls who are always discontented.

"I am going back to my nest," said the visiting Hen. "Perhaps the Man will bring me some Chickens too."

The Barred Plymouth Rock Hen sat on her nest in the carriage house, eating and drinking when she wished, and cuddling her children under her feathers. She was very happy, and thought it a beautiful world. "I would rather have had them gray," she said to herself, "but if they couldn't be gray, I prefer white. They are certainly Plymouth Rock Chickens anyway, and the color does not matter, if they are good."

She stood up carefully and took a long look at her family. "I couldn't have hatched out a better brood myself," she said.

"It is a queer thing for tables to take to hatching Chickens, but if that is the way it is to be done on this farm, it will save me a great deal of time and be a good thing for my legs. It is lucky that this Man came here. The Farmer who left would never have thought of making a table sit on eggs and hatch them."

THE MAN BUILDS A POULTRY-HOUSE

It would be wrong to say that all the poultry on the farm really liked the Man. The White Cock and the Brown Hen had never been known really to approve of anybody, and the Shanghai Cock was not given to saying pleasant things of people. However, the Man certainly had more and more friends among the fowls on the place, and when the White Cock and the Brown Hen wanted to say what they thought of his ways, they had to go off together to some far-away corner where they could not be overheard. If they did not do this, they were quite certain to be asked to talk about something else.

The five Hens who had had Chickens given to them were his firmest friends. It is true that each of them had really been on the nest long enough to hatch out Chickens of her own, yet they saw that another time they would be saved the long and weary sitting. They remembered, too, the Man's thoughtfulness in putting food and water where they could reach it easily on that first day, when they disliked so much to leave their families. They had spoken of this to the Gander, and had tried to make him change his mind about the fat table in the cellar. They might exactly as well have talked to a feed-cutter.

"I hear what you say," he replied politely (Ganders are often the most polite when they are about to do or say mean things). "I hear what you say, but you cannot expect me to change my mind about what I have seen with my own eyes. It was certainly quite wrong for him to get ready to burn those eggs, and the marking of them was almost as bad. As for this nonsense about the table hatching out Chickens, that is quite absurd. You could not expect a Gander to believe that. It is the sort of thing which Hens believe."

So the Man's friends had to give up talking to the Gander. Even the Geese were not sure that it was all right. "We would like to think so," they often remarked, "but the Gander says it cannot be."

Now the fowls had something new to puzzle them, for the Man spent one sunshiny morning in walking to and fro in the fields which had always been used for a pasture, stopping every now and then to drive a stake. Sometimes he walked with long strides, and then when his Little Girls spoke to him he would shake his head and not answer. Afterward he seemed to be measuring off the ground with a long line of some sort, letting the Little Girls take turns in holding one end of it for him.

After all of the stakes had been driven, the Man harnessed Brownie to the old stone-boat and began to draw large stones from different parts of the farmyard and pasture. He even went along the road and pried out some which had always lain there, right in the way of every team that had to turn aside from the narrow track. All these were drawn over to the stakes and tumbled off on the ground there.

In the afternoon the Farmer from across the road brought a load of lumber, which he left beside the stone and stakes, and then the work began. The Farmer, who was used to building barns and sheds, began to help the Man lay stone for some sort of long, narrow building. For days after that the work went on. Sometimes the two Men worked together, and sometimes the Farmer drove off to town for more lumber, after showing the Man just what to do while he was gone. The Man seemed to learn very easily, and did not have to take out or do over any of his work. That was probably because he listened so carefully when the Farmer was telling him. People always make mistakes, you know, unless they listen carefully to what they are told.

The poultry strolled around and discussed the new building every day. They could not imagine what it was to be. At first, when only the foundation was laid, it looked so long and narrow that the Gander declared it must be for a carriage house. "Don't you see?" he said. "There will be plenty of room for the platform wagon, the light lumber wagon, and the implements. When they are all in, there will be room for the Man to walk along on either side of them and clean them off. It is about the most sensible thing that I have known the Man to do." The Farmer always left his implements out in all kinds of weather, and sometimes one of his wagons stood out in a storm too.

Nobody except the Geese agreed with the Gander, and they would have agreed with him just as quickly if he had said that the building was for Barn Swallows. You see the Gander was always ready to tell what he thought, and as the Geese never even thought of thinking for themselves, it was very easy for them simply to agree with him.

Brown Bess looked at the long lines of stone all neatly set in cement, and said that she would not mind having one end of the building for herself and the Calf. "It would be much snugger than my place in the barn," said she, "although that is all right in warm weather."

Brownie may have known what it was for, because he had a great deal of Horse sense, but if he knew he did not tell. Being the only Horse on the place, and so much larger than any of the other people, he had not made friends very quickly, although everybody liked him as well as they had Bobs.

It was not until the Barred Plymouth Rock Hen saw that the long space was to be divided into many small rooms that she guessed it might be for the poultry themselves. Even then she dared not tell anybody what she thought. "In the first place," she said to herself, "they may prefer to run all over the farm, as they always have done, laying their eggs wherever they can. If any of them feel that way, they won't like it. If they really want a good house to live in, I might better not tell them what I think, for if I should be mistaken they would be disappointed." In all of which she was exactly right. It is much better for people not to tell their guesses to others. There is time enough for the telling of news when one is quite sure of it.

As the work went on, the Barred Plymouth Rock Hen noticed that at each end of the long space there was a sort of scratching-shed with an open front. The distance between these end sheds was filled by two closed pens, two more scratching-sheds, two more pens, and so on. There were doors from one room to another all the way along, big doors such as Men need, and there were little doors from each pen to its scratching-shed just large enough for fowls.

The Barred Plymouth Rock Hen grew more and more sure that her guess was right, and still she said nothing, although she was happy to see how warm and snug the Man was making the pens. "Why," she said to herself, "if he will let me live in that sort of house I will lay eggs for him in the winter." She had hardly got the words out of her bill when the other poultry came up. It was growing late, and they came for a last look at the house before going to roost.

"I declare," said the Gobbler, "I believe that house is for the Hens!"

"Surely not," said the Gander. "You don't mean for the *Hens*, do you?"

"That is what I said," replied the Gobbler, standing his feathers on end and dragging his wings on the ground. "Why not? The Man knows that Turkeys do not care much for houses, else we might have a place in it. I really wouldn't mind staying in a quiet home sometimes, but in pleasant weather my wives will go, and of course I cannot let them walk around the country alone, so that is how I have to spend my days."

The Turkey Hens looked at each other knowingly. They wished that he would leave them and their children quite alone. He was not fond of children, and the year before the Turkey mothers had had dreadful times in trying to keep theirs out of his sight.

"Let us go inside and see what it is like," said the little Speckled Hen, leading the way. Not until they reached the very last pen did they see enough to make them sure that the Gobbler was right. There they found the perches in place, the nest-boxes ready, and a fine feeding-trough just inside the large front window, where they could stand in the sunshine in winter and eat comfortable meals. The Cocks flew up at once to try the perches. "Fine!" said the Shanghai Cock. "Fine! These perches exactly fit my feet. I am glad that he made them large enough. Low, too, so that we cannot hurt ourselves in flying down."

"I like this," said the White Cock. "The perches are all the same height from the floor. I like a low perch, but not if other fowls are above me. Now you larger fellows can't roost any higher than I do. Cock-a-doodle-doo!" It is not strange that he crowed over it, because every night the fowls had been fighting for the highest roosting places, and the strongest were sure to win.

"Nests!" cackled the Hens. "Nests! How pleasant this will be! They are all in a row, so we can visit with each other while we are laying."

"That is a good plan," said the Brown Hen, who really seemed pleased at last. "I am always thinking of things to say when I am laying, and there is hardly ever any other fowl near enough to hear. It has been very annoying."

"I don't care so much about that," said a very sensible White Hen. "I can stand it not to talk for a while. What I want is a warm nest where the rain cannot strike me, and where I shall have quite room enough for my tail."

"That is what we want, too," said three or four others.

"There have always been so many unpleasant things," said the Brown Hen. "I have tried many places. I find a warm one where the wind cannot blow upon me, and usually there is not enough room for my tail. No Hen can lay comfortably in a nest when her tail is pushed to one side. I have tried laying under the currant bushes in warm weather, and there one has all out-of-doors for her tail, but on rainy days one has to change. I do not like changes."

"You do not?" asked the Shanghai Cock. "I thought all fowls liked changes. If you live here in winter, you will be walking from the pen to the scratching-shed half of the time."

"You know very well what I mean," said the Brown Hen. "I like the changes that I like, of course. Any fowl does. What I do not like is the changes that I don't like." She said this in a dignified and truly Hen-like manner, and then she walked off.

"All I hope," said the White Cock, sadly, "is that we shall not be shut up in these places during the summer. One cannot tell what may happen. One must expect the worst. When I see the wire front of the scratching-shed, I fear that we shall be kept in."

"Nonsense!" cried the Shanghai Cock. "Don't be a Goose. The Man has begun to put a wire fence around a great yard outside, and there will be plenty of room to run there if we are to live here. I do not believe that we shall be shut in, in pleasant weather."

"Come," clucked the Barred Plymouth Rock Hen to her brood. "Come with me to the carriage house. It is time all good little Chickens were asleep."

She was very happy over the pleasant things which she had heard said about the Man. Only a truly polite Hen could have kept from saying "I told you so," all this time, but she had shut her bill tightly and kept back the words she wanted to say.

You remember that the Shanghai Cock had always liked the Barred Plymouth Rock Hen, and now he thought she should be told how they had come to feel about her friend, the Man. He was not used to saying pleasant things, but having praised the perches made it a little easier for him. You know saying one kind thing always makes it easier to say another. So he ran after her.

"Er-er! I don't want the Farmer to come back," he said. Then he thought that did not sound quite right and he tried again. "I'm not sorry he went away. I mean I'm glad that the Man came. All of us are now, except the Gander and the White Cock, and you don't really care for them, do you?"

He looked at her lovingly with his round eyes, and the wind waved his drooping tail feathers. The Barred Plymouth Rock Hen thought that she had never seen him look so handsome. "I don't care at all about them," she replied quite honestly, "and I am glad that you and the others like the Man."

She said "you" much more loudly than she said "the others," and the Shanghai Cock must have known what she meant, for he stretched his neck, opened his bill, and gave such a crow as he was never known, before or since, to give at that hour of the day.

The Barred Plymouth Rock Hen went happily to her nest, and stayed awake long after her last Chicken was fast asleep. Even if one is grown-up and the mother of a family, even if one comes of a finer breed than one's neighbors, he cannot be truly happy without their hearty liking. This Hen felt that she had it at last, and that just by doing the thing which she thought right, but which the other poultry had not liked at all at first. It is often so.

THE PEKIN DUCK STEALS A NEST

THE Ducks were not much interested in the new poultry-house. To be sure the Hens talked of hardly anything else now, and several had said that they would be glad to lay in the new nest-boxes as soon as they should be lined with hay for them. So the Ducks heard enough about the house, but did not really care for it at all.

"It is too far from the river," said they. "We are quite contented with the old Pig-pen. Since the Hog and her children were taken away and the Man has cleaned it out, we find it an excellent place. There is room for all of us in the little shed where the Hog used to live, and the Man has thrown in straw and fixed good places for egg-laying. Besides, there is no door, and we can go in and out as often as we choose."

That was exactly like the Ducks. They seemed to think that to go where they wished and when they wished was the best part of life. The best part of sleeping in the old Pigpen, they thought, was being able to leave it whenever they chose. They knew perfectly well, if they stopped to think about it, that a Weasel or Rat could get in quite as easily as they, and it was only their luck which had kept them safe so long.

The Ducks were very pleasant people to know. They never worried about anything for more than a few minutes, and had charmingly happy and contented ways. There were only a few of them on the farm, and no two exactly alike in color and size. The Farmer had never paid much attention to them, and the Boy, who bought and kept them for pets, had tired of them so soon that they had been allowed to go wherever they pleased, until they expected always to have their own way.

They took their share of the food thrown out for the poultry, and then went off to the river for the day. During the hot weather they stayed there until after all respectable Hens had gone to roost. Even the Geese left the water long before they did. When they went to sleep, they settled down on the floor and dozed off. "It is much easier than flying up to roosts and then down again," they said. "Find a place you like, and then stay there. We see no reason why people should make such a fuss about going to sleep."

When the Shanghai Cock heard these things, he shook his head until his wattles swung. "That is all very well for the Ducks," said he, "but from the way this Man acts, I think there may be a change coming for them by and by. I notice that things are more different every day."

The Ducks soon began to see that it was different with them. Ducks, you know, are always very careless about where they lay their eggs. Some of these were so old that they seldom laid eggs, only the Pekin Duck and her big friend, the Aylesbury Duck, laid them quite often after the middle of winter. At first the Man looked in the old Pig-pen for them, but after he had looked many days and found only one, he drew a book out of his pocket and read a bit. Then he called the Little Girls to him and talked to them. "I want you to watch each of those white Ducks," said he, "and for every one of their eggs which you find I will give you a penny."

Each morning for some days after that, the two Ducks were followed by two hopeful Little Girls. "I don't mind it so much now," the Pekin Duck said to her friends on the third day, "but at first I didn't know what to do. I would no sooner sit down to lay under a bush or in some cosy corner than a Little Girl would sit on the ground in front and watch me. Then I would move to another place, and she would move too. I must say, however, that they are very good children. The Boy who lived here often threw stones at us. These children never do. I sometimes think there may be as much difference in Boys and Girls as there is in Ducklings."

When the Little Girls tired of watching for eggs to be laid, the Pekin Duck decided to do something she had never tried before. She was the youngest of the flock, and she wanted Ducklings. The older Ducks tried to discourage her. "Have a good time while you can," said the Aylesbury Duck, who was about her age, and thought Ducklings a bother. "I don't want to be troubled with a lot of children."

The old Ducks advised her not to try it. "You think it will be very fine," said they, "but you will find that you cannot go wherever you want to, and do whatever you please with Ducklings tagging along. The sitting alone is enough to tire a Duck out."

"Oh, I think I could stand it," remarked the Pekin Duck, quietly. "Didn't some Duck stand it long enough to hatch me?"

"Hatch you? No indeed," laughed an old Rouen Duck, who could remember quite distinctly things which had happened three years before on the farm from which they had all come to this. "Hatch you? A Shanghai Hen hatched you and half a dozen other Ducklings in a box with hay in it and slats across the front. I remember quite well how cross she became when she thought it time for her Chickens to chip the shell, and they did not chip. She never dreamed that she was sitting on Ducks' eggs, although every Duck on the place knew it and thought it a good joke. She was a stupid thing, or she would have known without being told. Any bright Hen knows that Ducks' eggs are larger, darker, and greasier looking than her own."

The Pekin Duck remembered very little of her life before coming to the farm, so she was glad to hear of it from the old Rouen Duck. "What did my mother do when her eggs didn't hatch?" said she.

"Do?" repeated the Rouen Duck. "Do? Why she did the only thing that any sitting fowl can do. She kept on sitting."

"How long?" asked the Pekin Duck.

"You don't suppose I can remember that, do you?" replied the Rouen Duck, twitching her little pointed tail from side to side. "Besides, I never count things. All I know is that she said one of the Cocks, who was a friend of hers, declared that the moon was quite new when she began sitting, and that she sat there until it was quite new again. He was roosting in a tree just then, and knew more about the moon because he always awakened to crow during the night. She thought it was dreadful to have to sit so long."

The Pekin Duck saw that the Rouen Duck was still trying to discourage her. "I suppose it was harder for her because her legs were longer," she said. "If they were longer they would ache more, wouldn't they?"

The Rouen Duck smiled all around her bill "Your mother had her worst time later on, though," she said. "When you and your brothers and sisters were hatched, she could not understand why you were so different from all the other children she had ever raised. She said that not one of you looked like her family, and the Shanghai Cock was very disagreeable to her about it. He said she should be more careful whose eggs she hatched. And when you children went into the water, your mother would walk up and down the bank of the pond, clucking as hard as she could, and begging you to come ashore at once. At night, too, there was trouble, for you would never go to bed as early as she thought proper. After a while she learned to march off at a time that suited her, and let you come when you were ready."

"Thank you ever so much for telling me," said the Pekin Duck, sweetly. "It must be horrid to have the wrong kind of children. I promise you that I will not sit on Hens' eggs." Then she waddled away.

"I want some Ducklings," said she, putting her pretty webbed feet down somewhat harder than usual. "I want Ducklings, and I am going to steal a nest at once." She was a Duck of determination, and made a start by finding a cosy spot under some burdock plants and laying an egg before she went in swimming. She was in such haste to make a beginning that she had actually to come back later to finish her nest, which she did by adding more dried leaves and grass and lining it with down which she plucked from her breast.

After that, of course, all her friends knew that it was useless to talk to her about it, for when a Duck goes around at that season of the year with her breast all ragged from her plucking it, people may be very sure that she is planning to hatch a brood. It is not at all becoming, but it is a great help, for when the sitting Duck is tired or hungry, she can pull the down over the eggs and leave her nest, knowing that the down will keep them warm for a long time.

Of course the other Ducks talked about her a good deal when she was not around, and said she would be sorry she had undertaken all that work and care, and that it was exactly as well to drop one's eggs anywhere and let the Man pick them up to put under some sitting Hen. "Yes," said the Aylesbury Duck, "or else give them to the fat table for hatching." Then they all laughed. It seemed such a joke to them that a table should take to hatching eggs.

Nearly every day the Pekin Duck laid an egg, and she soon had enough to begin sitting. After that, she did not go up to the Pig-pen at night with her friends. It was quite lonely in the clump of burdocks, and if the Pekin Duck had been at all timid she might have had some bad nights, for Weasels, Rats, and Skunks were out after dark, looking for something to eat. Yet they must always have found food before they reached the burdocks, for the Duck was not disturbed. During the day her friends came along for a chat, and often the Drake waddled up for a visit. He seemed to think her a very sensible sort of Duck. He had not the

Gobbler's dislike of children, although he never shared the labor of hatching them, like his friend the Gander. He thought one could be a good father without going quite as far as that.

The days were long and the nights seemed longer to the tired Pekin Duck, but her courage never failed. When her legs cramped so that she could hardly step off the nest, she smiled and said to herself, "Suppose I were a Thousand-Legged Worm!" She fancied it made her feel better to think of such things, and she never remembered that Thousand-Legged-Worms do not sit on nests and hatch out their children in that way. It is probably better that she did not. If it does one good to think of Thousand-Legged-Worms, it is wise to think about them, even if one does make a slight mistake of this sort.

When the rain came, the burdock leaves kept off most of it, and the few drops which fell between the leaves rolled off the Duck's back without wetting her at all. That was because her feathers were so oily that the rain could not stay on them. Ducks, you know, always have on their water-proofs, and can slip in and out of the water at any time without getting really wet.

The pleasure which she missed most was seeing the changes which the Man was making in the upper end of the pasture. The Drake told her how great yards had been fenced in with wire netting, and how the fronts of the scratching-shed had been covered with somewhat finer netting of the same kind. "Not even a Weasel could get through it," he said. And then the Pekin Duck wished that the Man would fix a place for her Ducklings where Weasels could not get them. She had never feared such creatures for herself, but when she thought of her children she was afraid. That is always the way, since it is much easier for a mother to be brave for herself than for her children.

On a beautiful morning in the last of May, the Pekin Duck was repaid for all her patience and courage by having seven beautiful Ducklings chip the shell. They were even more beautiful than she had thought they would be, and she could not understand why her friends seemed no more impressed. To be sure they said that they were fine Ducklings and that they looked like their mother, and admired their dainty little webbed feet and their bills. They spoke of the beautiful thick down which covered them, and said that they were remarkably bright and strong for their age. And yet the Pekin Duck could see that they had not properly realized what wonderful creatures the Ducklings were.

It was when all the Ducks were gathered around to look at the Ducklings that one of the Little Girls came along with her doll. When she also saw the Ducklings, she was so excited that she hugged her doll tightly to her heart and ran off to find her father.

A few minutes later the Pekin Duck saw her precious babies lifted into a well-lined basket and carried off toward the house. She followed, quacking anxiously, and keeping as close to the Man as possible. Twice he lowered the basket to let her see that her children were quite safe.

The Man carried the basket to a place beside the new poultry-house, now all done, and quickly fixed the old down-lined nest, which the Little Girl had been carrying in another basket, into a fine coop. Next he put the nestlings into it and let the Pekin Duck cover them with her wings. He stretched fine wire netting across the front of the coop, and then the Pekin Duck was perfectly happy. Indeed it was not until the middle of the following night that she remembered she had not looked at the poultry-house at all.

It was rather disappointing not to be able to take her children in swimming for two days, but when she saw how carefully the Man fed them on bread and milk and other soft food, and how particular he was about having plenty of clean water for them to drink, she quite forgave him for keeping them there. The other Ducks came to tell her how to care for the Ducklings, to shake their sleek heads, and to tell her how unfortunate it was that she could not take the Ducklings in swimming at once. "You will need to know many things," said the old Rouen Duck, "and I will tell you if you will come to me every time that you are perplexed."

"Thank you," said the Pekin Duck. But she never went. She thought it just as well that a Duck who had never hatched out children should not be giving advice to people who had.

When the Ducklings were three days old, they were let out and started at once for the river. When their mother had to stop to speak to her friends on the way, they did not wait for her, but marched on ahead. All the fowls spoke admiringly of them, and the Pekin Duck was truly happy as she looked at her seven proper little Ducklings.

They were such bright children, too, waddling right down to the edge of the brook and slipping in without a single question as to how it should be done. Their mother followed after and showed them how she fed from the bottom, reach-

SHE FOLLOWED QUACKING ANXIOUSLY.

ing her head far down until she could fill her orange-colored bill with the soft mud from the bottom. There were many tiny creatures in the mud which were good to eat, and these she kept and swallowed, letting the mud pass out between the rough edges of her bill. If the water had been deeper, she could have showed them how she dived, staying long under water and coming up in a most unexpected place.

When they came out of the water and stood on the bank, their mother stretched herself up as tall as she could and preened her feathers. The seven little Ducklings stood as tall as they could and squeezed the water out of their down with their tiny bills, which seemed so much longer for them than their mother's did for her.

The Pekin Duck was much amused to see how the other Ducks flocked around her children. Indeed, she laughed outright once, when she heard the old Rouen Duck say to the White Cock, "Don't you think that our Ducklings are growing finely?"

Of course the Pekin Duck was ashamed of having laughed at any one so much older than she, so she stuck her head under her wing and pretended to be arranging the feathers there. When she drew it out again she was quite sober, but she was thinking "Our Ducklings! Our Ducklings! They may all call them that if it makes them happy to do so, but really they are my Ducklings, for I earned them, and they love me as they love nobody else."

THE NEW NESTS AND THE NEST EGGS

As might have been expected, the new poultry-house was no sooner finished than the fowls began to discuss who should live in the different parts. They could see no reason why they should not all run together, as they always had done. "Perhaps," the Black Hen had said, "the Man may put us all together and let the table's Chickens have pens to themselves."

"What?" said the Barred Plymouth Rock Hen, "put me in one pen and my Chickens in another? That would never do."

"You forget," said the Shanghai Cock very gently, "that by winter-time they will not need your care any more, and you will not wish to be with them so much." And that was true, for no matter how fond a Hen may be of her tiny Chickens, she is certain to care less for them when they are grown.

All the fowls were quite sure that they should have the best pen and yard, because they had been the longest on the place. After they had spoken of that, they had a great time in deciding which was the best pen. Part of the fowls wanted to be in the end toward the road, so that they could see all that went on there and look across to the other farm to watch their neighbors. The Cocks all preferred this. They liked excitement.

Some of the Hens wished to live in the pen next to the barn. "We are fond of the barn," they said. "We have been there so much, and have laid so many eggs there that it seems like home. We know that it is not so comfortable, but it seems like home."

However, the Cocks had their wish, and on the day when it was granted there was such a crowing from fence-tops as greatly puzzled the Man. He could not find anything in his books and papers to explain it, although he looked and looked and looked. At last one of the Little Girls told him what she thought, and she was exactly right. "It sounds to me as though they were just happy," she said. You see the Man had not lived long enough on a farm to understand the language of poultry very well, so he had much to learn. There are many people who think themselves quite wise and yet cannot tell what one of a tiny Chicken's five calls means, and there are some Men, even some fathers (and fathers need to know more than anybody else in the world, except mothers) who do not know that a Cock can say at least nine different things with the same cry, "Cock-a-doodle-doo!"

This Man was a father and had been a school-teacher, too, so he was not an ignorant Man, and after his Little Girl said that he decided to learn poultry-talk. It took some weeks, but you shall hear by and by how well he succeeded.

The Man wanted to teach the Hens to lay in the new nests, so that he would not have to spend much time in egg-hunting, and because he wished to be sure of finding the eggs as soon as they were laid. People should grow good as they grow old, you know, but it is not so with the eggs. The Man did not want to shut the fowls in during the warm weather, for then he would have to feed them more, and that would cost too much money, yet he opened this front pen with its scratching-shed and yard, and fed them there every night. While they were feeding he closed the outer gate, so that they could not go back to roost on the trees or wherever they chose. The perches were comfortable, with room enough for all, and far enough apart so that those in the back rows did not have their bills brushed by the tails of those in front.

The Hens who had Chickens were now kept in the second pen from this, and so were quite safe from prowling Weasels and other hunters. In the front pen, you see, there were only full-grown fowls, and morning was a busy time for most of the laying Hens. The gate was not opened until the sun was well up, and by that time many of the Hens had laid in one of the cosy nests under the perches, nests which were so well roofed over that not even a pin-feather could have dropped into them from above. They were so very comfortable that even the Hens who did not lay before leaving the pen were soon glad to come strolling back to it, instead of fluttering and scrambling to some lonely corner of the hayloft in the barn.

On the first morning that the fowls were shut in there, a very queer thing happened. The first Hen to go on a nest exclaimed, "Why, who was here ahead of me?"

Nobody answered, and the Hen asked again.

At last the Speckled Hen said, "I think you are the first one to lay this morning."

"The first one!" exclaimed the Black Hen, for it was she, as she backed out onto the floor again. "You must not expect me to believe that I am the first when there is an egg in the nest already." As she spoke she pointed in with her bill, and the others came crowding around.

There lay a fine, large, and quite shiny egg. While they were still looking and wondering which Hen had laid it, the Brown Hen discovered that there was an egg in each of the six other nests. She was so excited that for a minute she could hardly cackle. The Black Hen began to look angry, and stood her feathers on end and shook herself in a way that she had when she was much displeased. She was not a good-natured Hen.

"You think that you are very smart," she said, "but *I* think that you are very silly. Every fowl here knows that I always like to be the first on the nest in the morning, and yet seven of you must have laid in the night to get ahead of me. I don't mind having an egg in the nest. Every Hen likes to find at least one there. It is the mean way in which you tried to prevent my getting ahead of the rest of you."

The Hens insisted that they never took their feet from the perches all night long, and the Speckled Hen, who was a very kind little person, tried to show the Black Hen that it was all a mistake of some sort. "Perhaps they were laid in there yesterday," said she, "only we did not notice them when we came in."

The Cocks kept still, although they looked very knowing. They did not want to offend any of the Hens by taking sides. At last the Brown Hen spoke. It always seemed that she made some trouble every time she opened her bill. "I remember," said she, "that there was not an egg there when I went to roost last night. The last thing I did before flying up onto my perch was to look in all the nests and try to decide which I preferred."

Then there was more trouble, and in the midst of it the Speckled Hen hopped into one of the nests. "Sorry to get ahead of you," she said politely to the Black Hen, "but the truth is that I feel like laying." She gave a little squawk as she brushed against the egg there. "It is light!" she cried. "It is light and slippery! None of us ever laid such an egg as that."

"Of course not," said one of the Cocks, who now saw his way to stop the trouble. "Of course none of you lay that sort of eggs. I could have told you that long ago, if you had asked me."

When the fowls were all looking at each other and wondering what sort of creature it could be who had slipped in and laid the eggs there, a tiny door in the outside wall, just back of one of the nests, was opened, and the Man peeped in. All he saw was a number of fowls standing around and looking as though they had been very much surprised. Half of the Hens stood with one foot in the air. He dropped the door, which was hinged at the top, and then the fowls looked at each other again. It was a great comfort to them at times like these to be able to look both ways at once. "The Man opened those little doors while we were asleep, and put those eggs in," they said. "They are not Hens' eggs at all. Probably they are some that his table laid."

It was only a minute before all the nests were in use, and soon the noise of puzzled and even angry clucking was replaced by the joyous cackling of Hens who felt that they had done their work for the day. "Of course," said the Speckled Hen, "those eggs cannot be so good as the ones we lay, but I do not mind the feeling of them at all. And I must say that finding them already in a strange nest makes it seem much more homelike to me. This Man acts as though he really understood Hens and wanted to make them happy."

THE WHITE PLYMOUTH ROCKS COME

Only a few days after the new poultry-house had been opened to the fowls on the place, the Man came home from town with a crate in his light wagon. In the crate were a Cock and ten Hens. All were very beautiful White Plymouth Rocks, and larger than any of the fowls on the place would have supposed possible. You can imagine what a scurrying to and fro there was among those who had always lived on the place, and how many questions they asked of each other, questions which nobody was able to answer.

"Are they to live on this farm?" said one.

"It must be so," answered another. "Don't you see that the Man is getting ready to open the crate?"

"Where do you suppose they came from?" asked a third. "Why, they are almost as big as Turkeys."

"Altogether too large, I think," said a Bantam. "It makes fowls look coarse to be so overgrown."

"What is that?" asked the Shanghai Cock, sharply. He had come up from behind without the Bantam's seeing him, and she hardly knew what to answer. She lowered her head and pecked at the ground, because she did not know what to say. She dared not tell the Shanghai Cock, who was very tall, that she thought large fowls looked coarse. So she kept still. It would have been much better if she had held up her head and told the truth, which was that she disliked to have large fowls around, since it made her seem smaller.

"I think," said the Shanghai Cock, "that if a fowl is good, the more there is of him the better. If he is not good, the smaller he is the better." He looked over towards the wagon as he spoke, but the Bantam knew that he meant her, and then she was even more uncomfortable. She thought people were all looking at her, and she felt smaller than ever.

The Man backed the wagon up to the outer gate of the second poultry-yard, which was just between the one where the Chickens were with their mothers and the one into which the older fowls were allowed to go. Then he loosened the side of the crate very carefully and took the new-comers out, one at a time. He had to hold the side of the crate with his hand, so the only way in which he could lift the fowls out was by taking them by the legs in his other hand and putting them, head downward, into the yard. One would think that it might be quite annoying to a fowl to have to enter his new home in that fashion, with all the others watching, but the White Plymouth Rocks did not seem to mind it in the least. Perhaps that was because they had been carried so before and were used to it. Perhaps, too, it was because they felt sure that the fowls who were standing around had also been carried by the legs. Perhaps it was just because they were exceedingly sensible fowls and knew that such things did not matter in the least. At all events, each Hen gave herself a good shake when allowed to go free, settled her feathers quickly, and began to walk around. The Cock did the same, only he crowed and crowed and crowed, as much as to say, "How fine it is to be able to stretch once more! A fellow could not get room to crow properly in that crate."

Now everybody knows that the poultry who had been long on the place should have spoken pleasantly to the White Plymouth Rocks at once. It would have made them much happier and would have been the kind thing to do. They did not do it, and there were different reasons for this. The Shanghai Cock was so used to saying disagreeable things every day to the fowls whom he knew, that now, when he really wanted very much to be agreeable, he found he did not know how. There are many people in the world who have that trouble. The Bantam Hen was cross, and walked away, saying to herself, "I guess they are big enough to take care of themselves." And that was a mistake, as you very well know, for nobody in this world is big enough to be perfectly happy without the kindness and friendship of others.

As for the rest of the fowls, some of them didn't care about being polite; some of them didn't know what was the best thing to say and so did not say anything; and some thought it would not do to talk to them, because they were not so large and fine-looking as the White Plymouth Rocks. They really wanted to do the kind thing, but were afraid they did not look well enough. As though kindness were not a great deal more important than the sort of feathers one wears!

The White Plymouth Rocks did the best that they could about it. They chatted pleasantly among themselves, saying

TOOK THE NEW-COMERS OUT, ONE AT A TIME.

that it was a fine day, and that it seemed good to set foot on grass once more, and that they had sadly missed having a bit of grass to eat with their grain and water while they were in the crate.

It was at this time that the Barred Plymouth Rock Hen in the next yard came over to the wire netting which separated the two. She would have come sooner if it had not been for her Chickens. Two of them had been quarrelling over a fat bug which they found, and she stayed to settle the trouble and scold them as they deserved. Now she came stepping forward in her very best manner to greet the strangers. She knew that she was not so large as they, and that her barred gray feathers were not nearly so showy as their gleaming white ones, but she also knew that somebody should welcome them to the farm, and she was ashamed that it had not been done sooner.

"Good-morning," said she. "I am very glad that you have come here to live."

"Oh, thank you," replied all the White Plymouth Rocks together. "We are very glad to meet you. We hope to be happy here."

"Have you come far?" asked the Barred Plymouth Rock Hen.

"Very far," said they. "Unless you have taken such a journey you can have no idea how glad we are to be free again."

"I have never taken any journey," said she, "except the time I came here to live, and that was when I was only a Chicken. I do not remember much about it. I fluttered out of a crate that was being carried in a wagon, and ran around alone until I happened to find this place."

"How sad!" exclaimed the Cock. "I hope you have had no such hard time since. They seem to have a good poultry-house here, although I have not yet been inside."

"It is a good one," said the Barred Plymouth Rock Hen, "but I do not sleep in it these warm nights. I stay in a coop in my yard with my children." As she spoke she looked lovingly down at the white flock around her feet. They were growing finely and already showed some small feathers on their wings.

"Oh!" exclaimed the Hens in the other yard. "Oh, what beautiful Chickens! So strong! So quick! So well-behaved! How long is it since you hatched them?"

"Well," replied their mother, "I suppose I did not hatch them. I sat long enough on the nest and laid enough eggs, but the Man who owns the farm took away my eggs and brought me these Chickens. He has a sort of table down in his cellar which hatches out all the Chickens on the farm. I might just as well have saved myself all those tiresome days and nights of sitting if I had known how it would be."

"That is a good thing to know," said one of the new-comers. "On the farm from which we came, all the Chickens are hatched in that way. We never had a mother who was alive."

"Not until after you were hatched I suppose," remarked the Barred Plymouth Rock Hen, who thought the other did not mean exactly what she had said.

"We had no real mother then," said the White Plymouth Rock Hen. "There were so many of us that we had to get along without. The Man who owned us had a lot of things to take the place of mothers. They were made of wood and some soft stuff and he used to set them around in the yards on pleasant days. We ate the food and drank the water that were brought to us, and then we played around in the grass near the make-believe mothers. When we were tired or cold we crawled under them and cuddled down, and when we were scared we did the same way. We were very well cared for by the Men, and we all grew to be strong and healthy fowls, but I sometimes wish that we could have had a live mother to snuggle under and to love."

The Barred Plymouth Rock Hen was greatly surprised. "I think it is well to save the Hens having to hatch out the broods," she said, "but they should be willing to care for the Chickens. There is nothing quite so good as a live mother."

Another Plymouth Rock Hen strolled up. "I have been in the pen and the scratching-shed," said she, "and I think them delightful."

"Are they at all like what you had before coming here?" asked the Barred Plymouth Rock Hen.

"Very much the same," was the reply. "Only on the farm from which we came there were a great, great many more pens. It took four Men to care for us all. Most of us were White Plymouth Rocks. What are those fowls outside? We never saw any that looked just like them."

"Oh," replied the Barred Plymouth Rock Hen with a little smile, "they don't know exactly what they are. The Shanghai Cock is a Shanghai, as any one can tell by looking at his long and feathery legs, but he and I are the only ones who belong to fine families. He is really an excellent fellow, although, of course, being a Shanghai is not being a Plymouth Rock."

"Of course not," agreed all the new fowls, speaking quite together. "We understand perfectly. You mean that he is a very good Shanghai."

"Exactly," said the Barred Plymouth Rock Hen. "The other fowls think him rather cross, but he never has been cross to me. I think he gets tired of hearing some of them quarrel and fuss, and then he speaks right out."

"One has to at times," said the Cock, politely, for he saw that the Barred Plymouth Rock Hen wished him to like her friends. "When you can," he added, "tell him that I would like to meet him. I suppose we shall not be allowed to go out of our own yard, but he can come up to the fence. And send the others also. We would like to meet our new neighbors."

"I will," replied the Barred Plymouth Rock Hen, as she clucked to her Chickens. "Good-by. I see that we have fresh food coming."

While her children were feeding she pretended to eat, pecking every now and then at the food, and chatting softly with them as they ate. There was always much to say about their manners at such times, and she had to use both of her eyes to make sure that they did not trample on the food. She also had to remind them often about wiping their bills on the grass when they had finished. She could not bear to see a Chicken running around with mush on the sides of his bill.

When they had eaten all they wished and ran away to play, she ate what was left and sat down to think. "I would like to be white," she said to herself. "I would certainly like to be white, and live in style with those fowls who have just come. It must be lovely to be so important that one is taken riding on the cars and lifted around carefully in crates."

Then she remembered how they had spoken of their legs aching, and how glad they were to be free on the grass once more. "I don't know that I would really care about travelling," she added, "but I would like to live in such style with a lot of fowls of my own family."

She remembered what the Cock had said about their having to stay in their own yard, and she added, "But I would not want to have to stay always in the same place."

She thought a little while longer and laughed aloud. "I believe that I would really rather be just what I happen to be," said she. "I don't know why I never thought of that before."

You can see that she was a most sensible Hen. Many fowls never stop to think that if they were to change places with others, they would have to stand the unpleasant as well as the pleasant part of the change.

The little white Chickens came crowding up to their gray mother. "Tell us what made you laugh," they said. "Please tell us."

Her small round eyes twinkled. "I was laughing," she said, "just because I am myself and not somebody else."

"We don't see anything very funny about that," they exclaimed. "Who else could you be?"

The Barred Plymouth Rock Hen sent them off to chase a Butterfly, and went to call on her nearest neighbor. "I would like to tell them," she said, "but they are too young to understand it yet."

THE TURKEY CHICKS ARE HATCHED

SPRING was always an anxious time for the Hen Turkeys who wanted to raise broods. Raising children is hard work and brings many anxieties with it. The mother is so much afraid that they will take cold, or eat too much, or not get enough to eat, or take something that is not good for children. There is also the fear that they may be careless and have some dreadful accident. And, worst of all, there is always the fear that they may be naughty and grow up the wrong sort of people.

These cares all mothers have, but the Turkey mothers have another care which is really very hard to stand, for the Gobblers do not like their children and will try in every way to prevent the eggs from hatching. If a Gobbler sees one of the Hen Turkeys laying an egg, he will break the egg, and if he meets a flock of tiny Turkey Chicks he will peck and hurt, perhaps even kill, all that he can of them. That is why the Hen Turkeys on the farm had always been in the habit of stealing away to lay their eggs in some secret place. One had even raised a fine brood in the middle of a nettle-patch the year before. She had slipped away from her friends and from the Gobbler day after day until she had laid thirteen eggs, and then had begun sitting. She had to sit as long as the Ducks do, and that is for twenty-eight days. You can imagine how tired she became, and how many times she had kept very still, hardly daring to move a feather, because she heard the Gobbler near and feared he would find and break her precious eggs.

Now she began to feel like laying, and walked off to the nettle-patch once more. She thought that having had such good luck there before was a reason for trying it again. She had hardly laid her fine large egg there when the Man came softly along and picked her up by the legs. She flapped her wings and craned her head as far upwards as she could, yet he did not loosen his hold on her. He carried her carefully, but he carried her just the same.

When he reached the poultry-house, he put her in a pen by herself. Then he went off to the farmhouse with her newly laid egg in his pocket. You can imagine how sad she felt. If there is one thing that a Hen Turkey likes better than taking long walks, it is raising Turkey Chicks. In spite of the weariness and the anxiety, she is very fond of it. And now this one found herself shut in and without her egg. It is true that, besides the pen, she could go into the scratching-shed and the big yard, yet even then there was the wired netting between her and the great world, and her friends were on the other side of the fence. She was just wondering if she could not fly over the fence and be free, when the Man returned and cut some of the long feathers from her right wing. Then she knew that she could not fly at all.

The Man next made a fine nest of hay in a good-sized

box, placing it in the shed and putting an egg into it. The Hen Turkey first thought that it was her own egg, but when the Man left and she could come nearer, she found that it was not. Instead, it was different from any she had ever seen. She tried sitting on it. "It feels all right," she said in her gentle and plaintive voice. "If I am still here when I want to lay another, I will use this nest."

In spite of her loneliness and sadness, the Hen Turkey managed to keep brave during the days that followed. The Man gave her plenty of good corn and clean water, and she had many visits with the Hens and their Chickens who lived in the pen next to hers and ran about all day in their yard. Of course she did not think them so interesting as Turkey Chicks, yet she liked to watch them and visit with them between the wires. It made her want a brood of her own even more than ever.

She still laid eggs right along, and the Man took each away soon after it was laid. She feared that he took them to eat, but the Barred Plymouth Rock Hen said that he might be giving them to the table to hatch, and that she should not worry. "I had just such a time myself," she added, "and it all came out right. You see if he does not bring you some fine Turkey Chicks soon."

This always cheered the Hen Turkey for a time, but even if it were to be so, she thought, she would prefer to hatch her own eggs. She did not know that the Man had every one of hers in a basket in a dry, warm place in the house, and was turning each over carefully every day. This he did to keep them in the best possible way until there should be a nestful for her to sit on.

Sometimes the Gobbler and the two other Hen Turkeys came up to the fence to visit with her. They never stayed long, because they came of a restless and wandering family, yet it did her good to have chats with them, even if they walked back and forth part of the time as they talked. The Gobbler paid very little attention to her. He told her once that the Hen Turkeys who were foolish enough to try to raise broods deserved to be shut up and have their wings clipped. She had better visits with her sisters when he was not there to listen. One of them told her that she had several eggs hidden under a sumach bush in a fence corner. The other said that she was trying to decide on a nesting-place; she couldn't choose between a corner of the lower meadow and the edge of the woods. Both of them spoke very softly, and frequently looked over toward where the Gobbler was strutting in the sunshine. They were much afraid that he would hear.

When her sisters walked away, the Hen Turkey in the yard felt sadder than ever. She strolled back into the shed and tried to think of something pleasant to do. She had not laid an egg for two days, and she was very lonely. You can imagine how pleased and happy she was to see eleven fine Turkey eggs lying in her nest. The queer egg which she had not laid was gone, and she felt certain that those there were all her own. She got on the nest at once, and found that she could exactly cover them. "How lucky!" she thought. "If there were another one it would be too many and I could not keep it warm."

She did not know she had laid fifteen eggs, and that the Man had taken the other four down cellar to be hatched by the incubator. She thought it just luck that there were precisely enough. She did not know the Man had read in one of his books that a Hen Turkey can safely cover only eleven eggs. There are several things better than luck, you see. Willingness to study is one and willingness to work is another. This Man had both kinds of willingness, and it was well for his poultry that he had.

There is not much to be told about the days that passed before the first Turkey Chick chipped the shell. The sun shone into the open front of the shed for twenty-eight days, and the patient Hen Turkey was there, sitting on her nest. The moon shone into the shed for many nights, and she was still there. The moon could not shine in for twenty-eight nights for two reasons. Sometimes it set too early, and sometimes the nights were cloudy and wet, although none of the days were.

When it rained the Turkey was the happiest. She did not like wet weather at all. It was for this reason she was happy. Every shower reminded her how wet it must be out in the nettle-patch, and made her think how cosy and happy she was in the place which the Man had made ready for her.

Then came the joyous day on which ten little Turkey Chicks chipped the shell. They were very promising children, quite the finest, their mother thought, that she had ever seen. There was only one sad thing about the day, and that was not having the eleventh egg hatch. The Turkey Hen was too happy with her ten children to spend much time in thinking of the other which she had hoped to have, but she could not help remembering once in a while, and then she became very sad.

It was not until the next morning that the ten little ones began to eat and to run around. Young Turkeys do not eat at all the first day, you know, but they always make up for it afterwards.

When the Hen Turkey walked out of the shed with her family, the Hens in the next yard crowded to the fence to see them. The little White Plymouth Rocks could not understand for a long time why the Turkey Chicks should be so large. "It isn't fair," they said. "Those Turkey Chicks will be grown up long before we are!" They thought that to be grown up was the finest thing in the world.

The Hens were very friendly and chatted long about them, telling the fond mother how very slender their necks were and how neat their little feet looked, with the tiny webs coming half-way to the tips of their toes. "I am very glad for you," said the Barred Plymouth Rock Hen. "I was sure that it would all come out right in the end. This Man takes excellent care of his poultry."

After a while the Gobbler came strutting past. When he saw his children, he stood his feathers on end and dragged his wings on the ground. He was exceedingly angry, and would have liked it very well if they had been on his side of the fence.

"Ugly little things!" he said to their mother. "They will tag around after you all the rest of the summer."

"Very well," she replied. "I shall like to have them."

"Silly—silly—silly!" said the Gobbler, as he strutted off.

The Hen Turkey's sisters came walking slowly toward her. Both of them were sitting on eggs, and had left their nests for a few minutes to find food. Of course they could not make a long call. “I built in the edge of the woods after all,” said the one who had been so undecided. “I wanted you to know, but don’t tell anybody else, or the Gobbler may hear of it and find the nest.” Then she spoke of the ten Turkey Chicks and asked the other sister to notice how much they looked like their mother. After that they had to hurry back to their nests.

When the Hen Turkey called her Chicks to cuddle down for the night, she found four already in the shed, eating from the food-dish.

“I thought you were all outside with me,” she remarked. “Why did you come in here?”

“We couldn’t help ourselves,” said they. “Some very large creature brought us here just now. We came from a darker place than this.”

The mother was very much puzzled. She knew that she had not hatched them, and that they could not belong to her sisters, who had begun sitting after she did. There was no way of taking them to any other place for the night, so she decided to do the kind thing and care for them herself. She was quite right in this. One is never sorry for having done the kind thing, you know, but one is very often sorry for having done the unkind thing. “Crawl right under my wings,” said she, “and cuddle down with these other Turkey Chicks. I will try to cover you all.”

She managed very well and the night was warm, so that although a few of the Chicks were not wholly covered all the time, they got along very comfortably indeed. By the next morning the mother loved the four as much as she did her own ten. “It really doesn’t matter in the least who hatched them," she said, "or even who laid the eggs. They need a mother and I can love them all. It would be a shame if I couldn't stretch my wings a little more for the sake of covering them." She never knew that they had been hatched in the incubator from the four eggs which she had laid, but which the Man had thought she could not cover. You see she was really adopting her own children without knowing it.

Turkey mothers are hungry creatures, and do not understand that they should not eat the hard-boiled eggs which are the best food for their Chicks when very small. So the Man had either to shut this mother in the shed and place the food for the Chicks outside, where she could not reach it, or else find some other way of keeping it from her. He thought a Turkey who had sat so closely on her nest for four weeks should be allowed to stretch, so he put the food for the children in a coop and left the mother free. The little ones could run in and out whenever they wanted to eat, and the mother had plenty of corn and water outside, so they were all well cared for and happy. The Gobbler said unkind things to them each time he passed, but they were too happy and sensible to mind that very much, and it did not seem long before the Chicks' tail-and wing-feathers were showing through their down, and they were given porridge and milk instead of hard-boiled egg. This made them feel that they were growing up very fast indeed, and they kept stretching their tiny wings and looking around at their funny little tails to watch their feathers lengthen.

On the day when they had their first porridge, their aunts and their newly hatched cousins were brought in to share their yard with them. You can imagine what happy times they all had, playing together and visiting through the wire fence with their next-door neighbors, the White Plymouth Rock Chickens.

The Gobbler used to pass by and try to make them and their mothers unhappy by telling them of the pleasure they missed by being shut up. "There is fine food in the lower meadow," he said, "and the upper one is even better. There are delicious Bugs to be found by the side of the road. But these are for me, and not for silly Hen Turkeys and their good-for-nothing Chicks."

One day the outer gate of the empty yard next to theirs was left open and some fine corn strewn inside, just as the Gobbler came along. He strutted in to eat the corn, thinking a little of it would taste good before he started for the meadow.

He stood with his back to the gate while eating, and quite often he stopped between mouthfuls to tell the Hen Turkeys how fine it was outside. Soon he noticed the Man opening the gate of their yard and letting the oldest flock pass through with their mother. He took one hurried last mouthful and turned to leave. The gate of his yard was shut, and he was too fat and old to fly over the fence.

The happy Turkey mother paused on her way to the meadows with her flock. She was a very patient creature, and would never have dared say anything of the sort to the Gobbler when he was free, but now she decided to say what she wished for once. "Thank you very much for telling us about the fine food outside," said she. "We shall soon be enjoying it. We shall first try the lower meadow and then the upper one. After that we shall hunt for those delicious

THE HAPPY TURKEY MOTHER PAUSED ON HER WAY.

Bugs which you say may be found by the roadside. Probably we shall find plenty of dandelion, cress, and mustard leaves, with a few Ants or nettles to give flavor. It is really very fine outside."

THREE CHICKENS RUN AWAY

One would think that with such a good mother as the Barred Plymouth Rock Hen, Chickens should have been contented to mind her and follow wherever she went, and usually hers did. One day, however, two of the brothers coaxed their good little sister to go with them to visit the Chickens at the farm across the road. The brothers had teased and teased their mother to let them go there, but she had always refused.

"Why?" they said.

"Because," answered the Barred Plymouth Rock Hen, "you have enough room and enough playmates right here at home, and I know that you are safe and well here. I do not know what might happen to you there."

"Oh, *why* can't we go?" teased the brothers, who had just been given an answer to that same question, and were very rude to keep on asking it.

Of course the Barred Plymouth Rock Hen had had too much experience with Chickens to reply again to a question which should not have been asked the second time, and might better not have been asked the first. So she just turned her back and walked off, clucking to her brood as she went. The brothers who had been teasing did not like that at all, and they put their naughty little heads together and decided to run away.

"Let's get Little Sister to go along," said Older Brother.

"Why?" asked Younger Brother. "She can't run as fast as we can, and she's so good that it wouldn't be much fun anyway. We wouldn't get across the road before she'd want to come back and be afraid our mother would worry about us."

"That is just why I want her to go along," said Older Brother. "We'll get her to go, and then our mother will think that we are not any worse than she is, and perhaps she won't peck us so hard when we get back."

"All right," said Younger Brother, fluttering his wings with impatience. "Let's get her right now. I know our mother won't scold her."

You see both of the brothers forgot that the reason why their mother had never scolded Little Sister was that Little Sister had never done anything wrong. She was really the best Chicken in the brood, and she had such a sweet way of running to the Barred Plymouth Rock Hen during the day and cuddling close to her for a short rest, that it was not strange her mother was especially fond of her.

Now the two naughty brothers found Little Sister and began talking to her. "Ever been across the road?" asked Older Brother, carelessly, as he snapped off a blade of grass.

"No," said Little Sister. "Mother never goes."

"There are some very jolly Chickens on that farm," remarked Younger Brother. "One of them asked us to come over a little while ago."

"Wouldn't it be fun!" exclaimed Little Sister. "Let's ask Mother if we can't all go."

"Aw, they won't want the whole brood at once," said Older Brother. "Besides, our mother is way over in the edge of the pasture now, and there isn't any use in bothering her. I tell you what let's do. Let's just go down to our side of the road and see if those other Chickens are there now. Then we can ask them if they don't want us to come over some other day."

You see the brothers knew that it would never do to ask their sister to run away with them at first, for she would have said "No," and run off to tell the Barred Plymouth Rock Hen, and that would have spoiled all their naughty fun.

The three little White Plymouth Rocks put down their heads and scurried along as fast as they could toward the road. Older Brother planned it so that the fence should hide them from their mother as they ran, but he said nothing of this to Little Sister, for she was not used to being naughty, and he knew that he would have to go about it very carefully to get her to run away. When they reached the road they saw the Chickens on the other side, but they were well within their own farm-yard.

"Oh, isn't that too bad!" exclaimed Little Sister. "Now you can't ask them what you wanted to."

"We might run over and speak to them about it now," said Younger Brother. "Mother won't care. After we have come so far to see them, it seems too bad to miss our chance. Come on and we can be across before that team gets here." Both the brothers put down their heads and ran as fast as they could, and Little Sister followed after them. When they were on the other side she began to cry and wanted to go back.

"I n-n-never did such a thing in all my l-l-life," she sobbed, "and I know our mother won't like it. Let's go right back."

"Oh, don't act like a Gosling," said Older Brother. "You're over here now and you might as well have a good time. What if our mother does scold when we get back? She never wants us to have a bit of fun, and we're just as safe here as we were at home."

Little Sister did not feel at all happy, still, you know how hard it is to stop being naughty when you have once begun, and she found it hard. She would gladly have returned at once if her brothers had been willing to go with her, but when she found that they were going to stay, she stayed with them. The Chickens whom they were visiting were very jolly and full of fun, although they were of common families and had not been carefully brought up. They did many things which the little White Plymouth Rocks had never been allowed to do, and in a short time the visitors were doing just the same as they.

These Chickens even made fun of each other when they had accidents, and Little Sister heard them laughing at three or four who were acting as though they were sick and opening their bills very wide. "What is the matter with those Chickens?" she asked.

"Oh, they have the gapes," answered one of the Chickens who lived there, and then he began speaking of something else.

It is very sad to have to tell such a thing, but the truth

is that the three White Plymouth Rock Chickens did not return to their home until nearly roosting-time. Even Little Sister pecked and squabbled and acted like the rest. They walked up the tongue of a hay wagon that stood in the yard, and scrambled and fluttered until they were on the edge of the rack. "Dare you to fly down into the old hen-yard," said one of the Chickens who lived on the place. "We used to live in there until a few days ago, and then the Farmer turned us out and shut the gate after us."

"Why did he do that?" asked Older Brother.

"I don't know," was the answer. "Nobody knows why Farmers do things. I think he did it just to be mean. There were fine Angleworms in there, and now we can't get one of them. Dare you to fly down there! You can get out somehow."

Older Brother was not brave enough to refuse, so over he flew, and Younger Brother came after him. The other Chickens fluttered along with them and Younger Brother gave Little Sister a shove that sent her over the fence when he went. They found a great many Angleworms there, and ate and ate and ate, and tried to get the largest ones away from each other; but after a while the Farmer's Wife saw them and came running to shoo them out with her apron. Little Sister was really glad when this happened, for she had found no place where she could crawl through the fence. She would have told her brothers about it if she had not feared that they would laugh at her and call her a coward. She did not know that each of them was thinking the same thing and dared not speak of it for the same reason. Of course the Chickens who lived on that farm all the time did not care so much. Naughty Chickens, like the three little run-aways, are almost sure to think about their mothers when the sun begins to set and the shadows on the grass grow long. Then they begin to think about home, too, and wish that they did not have to be ashamed of themselves.

When these brothers and their sister got out of the hen-yard, they started straight for home. At first they ran, and quite fast too, but as they got nearer they began to go more slowly, and once in a while one of them would stop to peck at something or other. You see they were thinking of what the Barred Plymouth Rock Hen would be likely to say to them. They thought that they would find her in the old coop where they had lived when first hatched. They ran the fields now, yet always went back there to spend the nights.

They were trying so hard to find excuses for themselves that they did not notice the Barred Plymouth Rock Hen behind the stone-pile in the lane. She had got the rest of her brood settled in the coop for the night and then started out in search of the wanderers. As soon as they passed the stone-pile, she ducked her head and ran after them as fast as she could, dragging the tips of her wings on the ground and pecking at them hard and fast. You should have seen them run. They fluttered their wings wildly and never thought of making excuses. The one thing they remembered was that if they only reached the coop they could crawl in under their good brothers and sisters and be safe from their mother's bill.

Little Sister got punished as well as her brothers, and that was perfectly right. For she need not have gone with them, even if they did ask her. It may be that her mother did not peck her quite so hard as she did the others, but it was hard enough to make her glad to reach the coop at last.

The good Chickens were almost asleep when these three dived in under them, and it took some time for them all to get settled again. The Barred Plymouth Rock Hen sat down beside the pile of her children and looked very hot and severe, yet she did not scold them then.

The rest of the brood were sound asleep when Little Sister slipped out from under them to cuddle close to her mother. She could not sleep until she had confessed it all, and that shows that she was a good Chicken at heart. When she told about their getting into the closed hen-yard, and how they had been driven out of it, the Barred Plymouth Rock Hen looked very much startled. "Did any of your playmates over there go around with their mouths open?" said she.

"Oh yes," replied Little Sister. "A good many of them did, and the rest of us laughed at them." Then she drooped her head because she felt ashamed of having been so rude.

"I am afraid the punishment I gave you will be only a small part of it," said the Barred Plymouth Rock Hen; "but now you must go to sleep, and we will not talk any more of your naughtiness. You did quite right to tell me all about it."

THE THREE RUNAWAYS BECOME ILL

NOBODY can tell just how long it was after the Chickens ran away, but it was certainly some little time, when Older Brother began to have trouble about breathing. "There seems to be something stuck in my throat," said he to his mother. "I can't breathe without opening my mouth a good deal."

"There is something stuck in my throat too," said Younger Brother.

"And in mine," added Little Sister.

The Barred Plymouth Rock Hen looked very sad. "It is just as I expected," said she.

At that moment another brother ran up. "What's the matter with these Chickens?" he asked his mother. "They've been running around all morning with their mouths open, and it makes them look too silly for anything. I don't want to play with them if they can't keep their bills shut. I wish you'd tell them to stop."

"They can't stop," said the Barred Plymouth Rock Hen, sadly. "They have the gapes."

"What is that?" cried all the four Chickens together, while three of them looked badly scared.

"That is a kind of illness," answered their mother. "I have been expecting it all along."

"What did you let us be sick for then?" asked Older Brother. "Why didn't you tell us to eat more gravel or something? I don't think it is taking very good care of us to let us get sick."

"Now," said the Barred Plymouth Rock Hen, and she spoke very firmly, "you are not to speak again until you can speak properly. On the day you ran away you played with Chickens who had the gapes, and you went with them into a closed hen-yard and ate Angleworms. That is what gave you the gapes. There were tiny Gapeworms in the Angleworms, and you swallowed them. Now the Gapeworms are living in your throats and you cannot get them out. The Farmer had shut the poultry out of that yard because he knew that they would become ill if they fed in there. Now you are ill and I can't help you."

Older Brother looked scared. "How did she know what we did over there?" he whispered to Younger Brother.

"I don't know," answered Younger Brother, while he watched his mother to be sure that she did not overhear. "Mothers always seem to find out what a Chicken is doing, anyhow."

Little Sister began to cry. "I'm afraid we are going to die," she sobbed. "I feel so very, very badly."

"Shall we die?" asked the sick brothers, and they were so scared that their bills chattered. Their teeth would have chattered, you know, if they had had teeth, but none of their family ever do have them.

"Yes," answered their mother, sadly. "You will die unless

something is done to get the Gapeworms out of your throat. I cannot help you, for they cannot be taken out by creatures who have only wings and feet. There are times when hands would be handy. The only thing for you to do is to find the Man and keep near him until he sees that you are ill and does something to cure you. I will go with you."

You can imagine how sad the whole brood felt when they heard the news. The brother who had not wanted to play with them was much ashamed of himself, and kept scratching up fine Worms for the sick Chickens to eat. He thought that a good way of showing how sorry he felt.

"I tell you what," said Older Brother to Younger Brother. "If I ever get well again, I'll mind my mother every time, even if I just hate to!"

"So will I," said Younger Brother. "I wish we hadn't coaxed Little Sister to go along."

By this time they had reached the place where the Man was working. It seemed a long while before he noticed that three of them were sick. When he did, he put his hat on the back of his head and wiped his forehead with his handkerchief. His handkerchief was white. The Farmer had always carried red ones, and the Gobbler was much pleased when he found that the Man did not.

"I wonder what is the matter with those Chickens," said the Man. "They must be sick in some way. I will look it up in one of my books."

That was why, soon after this, the Man came from the house with a small book and seated himself on the wheel-barrow to read. He would look at the page for a few minutes, then put his finger on a certain part of it and watch the sick Chickens. At last he arose and put the book in his pocket. Then he got a box and a piece of burlap. He also had a pan with some white powder in it. He set these down close together and threw grain to the Chickens. When they came to pick it up he caught the sick ones and put them into the box. "Oh! Oh!" they cried. "Mother! Mother! The Man has caught us! The Man has caught us!"

"Keep still! Keep still!" clucked the Barred Plymouth Rock Hen. "The Man has to catch you before he can cure you." She spoke as though she was not in the least frightened, but the truth is that she was very badly scared. She could not stand still, and kept walking to and fro, clucking as fast as she could. She had never seen anybody use a box and powder for Chickens that had the gapes. The Farmer had always made loops of Horse-hair and put them down the Chickens' throats to catch and draw out the tiny Worms. That was bad enough, and always hurt the Chickens, but she had never told them beforehand that it would hurt. You can see that she was a very brave Hen, for she made her children stand the hard times that would make them better, and a Hen needs to be very brave for that.

Now the Man covered the open top of the box with burlap and began to sift the white powder through it.

"Ow!" said Older Brother, coughing as though he would never stop. "Ow! Ow! I can't breathe! I am stifling!"

"Ow!" said Younger Brother. "Ow! Ow! I can't stop coughing!"

"Ow!" said Little Sister. "Ow! Ow! Isn't this dreadful!"

The three Chicks staggered around in the box, coughing just as hard as they could. The dust which came down through the burlap seemed to bite and sting their throats, and very soon they were coughing so hard that they could not speak at all. The Man was coughing too, but he did not stop for that. The Chickens who were well could not understand what the Man was doing to the sick ones, and it was a very sad time for the whole family. At last the Man uncovered the box and lifted the Chickens out. They could not stop coughing all at once, yet they managed to get over to where their mother was. Then she spread her wings and tried to cover them, as she had done when they were first hatched. She could not do it, because they were so big; still, it comforted them to have her try, and after a while they were able to speak.

"Why," said Older Brother. "I must have coughed up some of the Gapeworms! I can breathe with my mouth shut."

"So can I," said Younger Brother.

"So can I," said Little Sister.

"Then come down to the meadow for the rest of the day," said their mother. "We can find good feeding there."

"We will come," answered the three, and they were hardly away from their mother's side during the rest of that day. Once they got near the fence that separated the meadow from the road, and a couple of Chickens from the other farm called to them to come across. "Uh-uh!" they answered. "Our mother doesn't want us to."

They did not even ask their mother what she thought

about their going, and there was no reason why they should, for they knew perfectly well that they ought not to go. When they had walked so far away that they were sure of not being overheard, they looked each other in the eye and said solemnly, "You don't catch us going where our mother thinks we should not!"

THE YOUNG COCK AND THE EAGLE

THIS is a sad story. It is not pleasant to tell sad stories, but if they were not told once in a while, people would never know what really happens in the world. And surely you would not wish to miss hearing of what was really the most exciting happening of all, during that first summer after the Man bought the farm.

You remember having heard something about the Young Cock. Before the coming of the White Plymouth Rocks, there had been only three Cocks on the farm. The Shanghai Cock was the oldest, and a very grumpy fowl, but quite sensible in spite of that. The White Cock was somewhat younger than the Shanghai, and was not a very strong fellow. He was always unhappy about something, and it was said that he did not eat enough gravel. If that was true, he should not have expected to be well, since his stomach would then have no way of grinding up his food and getting the strength out of it. The Young Cock was a strong and exceedingly conceited fellow. You probably know what conceited people are. They are the people who think themselves very clever, but who are not really so.

This last one was always called the Young Cock, because the other two were so much older than he, although by this time he was old enough to be over such foolishness as bragging and picking quarrels with others. He had feathers of many colors in his coat, and thought that one of his great-great-great-grandfathers had been a Game Cock. Game Cocks, you know, are often very beautiful to look at, and are great fighters. He was not really sure about any of his family except his mother, who had died the year before, and was a very common-looking Hen of no particular breed. However, he had thought and talked so much about Game Cocks that he had come really to believe in this great-great-great-grandfather. It is good to have fine grandparents, and it is good to remember them and try to be the right sort of grandchildren for their sakes, but having fine grandparents does not always make people themselves equally fine, and it is not wise to talk too much about what they have been. It is better to pay more attention to being what one should.

All summer the Young Cock had been growing more and more annoying in his ways. He made fun of everybody whom he did not like, and sometimes even of those whom he did. He crowed and strutted and strutted and crowed. He called the Barred Plymouth Rock Hen "an old fogy," and the Brown Hen "an old fuss." The Barred Plymouth Rock Hen was not an old fogy, but a middle-aged and very sensible fowl, and although the Brown Hen was quite fussy, she was older than the Young Cock, and he should not have spoken of her in that way.

He did not always go to roost quite as soon as the other fowls and, if he found one of them in the place which he wanted, he often pushed and shoved until he had the place and the other fowl landed on the floor. “Get off of there,” the Young Cock would say. “I want that place. Move along or get off!”

When he was really very young, the older fowls had hoped that he would outgrow his rude and quarrelsome ways, so they stood it much longer than they should. Now he was older and there was not a single excuse to be found for him. He might better have been punished for it when young, because then he would have been well-behaved when grown up.

One morning he fluttered down from his perch in a very bad temper. Some of the Pullets, or young Hens, had been making fun of him the night before and comparing him with the White Plymouth Rock Cock. They meant only to tease him, but it had made him cross, and he awakened even more cross after his night’s sleep. He decided to show those Pullets that he was not to be laughed at. He was thinking of this when he stalked out into the yard. Some of the White Plymouth Rock Chickens ran along on the other side of the wire fence, peeping prettily and wanting to talk with him.

“Go back to your mother,” he said. “What business have you to be tagging me around like this? I don’t want to talk to you. Chickens should not speak until they are spoken to. Run!”

Of course they ran. You would if you were a Chicken and a Cock should speak to you in that way. They ran to their mother, and it took her a long time to comfort them.

Next the Young Cock stepped directly across the path

of the Shanghai Cock, stopping him in his morning walk. The Hens who saw it done expected the Shanghai Cock to fight him on the spot, but they saw nothing of the sort. The Shanghai Cock did not think it worth while. The saucy Pullets were eating in a corner of the yard and chattering over their corn.

"Wouldn't it be fun to see the Young Cock get punished by the Shanghai?" one of them said.

"Why don't you like him?" asked another.

"I do like him," answered the first. "I like him very much, but he is conceited and brags so that I wish somebody would teach him a lesson."

"Look!" cried another. "He is picking a quarrel with the White Cock."

They looked and saw him standing in front of the White Cock with his head lowered, staring steadily at him. The White Cock looked as though he did not care to fight, but being no coward, he would not turn his tail toward the other and run away. He simply stood where he was, and whenever the Young Cock lowered his head the White Cock lowered his. Whenever the Young Cock gave a little upward jerk to his head, the White Cock did the same. At first he was only trying to protect himself and be ready for a blow if the Young Cock should begin to fight in earnest. Pretty soon he began to think that he would beat him if he could. He thought it might be a good time to teach him something. After that both fought as hard as they could, staring, ducking, bobbing, fluttering, pecking, and striking with their bills and the sharp spurs that grew on their legs. It ended by the White Cock staggering and running away from the blows, while the other stood proudly where he was and crowed and crowed and crowed.

The Young Cock did not beat because he understood the movements to be made any better than the other. He beat only because he was younger and stronger. He did not look toward the Pullets, feeling quite sure that they were looking toward him and admiring him. He flew onto the top rail of the pasture fence and crowed as loudly as he could. "Cock-a-doodle-doo!" said he. "I have beaten him! I have beaten him!"

The Shanghai Cock looked at him with great displeasure. "Something will happen to that young fellow some day," said he, "and after that he will not crow so much."

The Pullets heard him say this and were scared. They did not wish anything dreadful to happen to him. One of them wanted to tell the Young Cock what they had overheard, but the others would not let her.

It was not long after this, in fact it was before the Hens had come out of the large open gate of their yard, that the Young Cock picked up and ate a grain of corn which the Shanghai Cock had already bent over to eat. The older Cock did not like this, and he said so very plainly. The Young Cock lowered his head and looked the Shanghai Cock squarely in the eye. "If you don't like my way of eating," he said in his rudest tone, "you can try to punish me."

"I will try it with pleasure," replied the Shanghai Cock, and they stared and ducked and hopped and fluttered and jumped and struck at each other with feet and bill, until the Young Cock had really beaten the Shanghai. It should have been the other way, yet it was not, for the Shanghai was growing old and fat, and could not get around so quickly as the Young Cock.

Of course the Pullets were glad, but nobody else was. “There will be no getting along with him at all after this,” the Hens said. “If he had been well beaten for once, he might have learned manners.” They paid no attention to the Cocks who were beaten, for that would not be thought polite among fowls. Instead, they walked about as usual, pretending that they had not noticed what was going on, and twisting their necks, lifting their feet, and dusting themselves in the most matter-of-fact way.

The Young Cock flew onto the fence again. “Cock-a-doodle-doo!” said he. “Cock-a-doodle-doo! I can beat them all! I can beat them all!” He strutted back and forth there for a time, and then flew to the top of the old carriage-house. Here he strutted and crowed and crowed and strutted, while the fowls in the pasture below looked at him and wondered how he dared go so high.

Suddenly the Shanghai Cock, who had been quietly trying to arrange his feathers after the fight, saw a large, dark bird swooping down from the sky and gave a queer warning cry. “Er-ru-u-u-u-u!” he said. “Run! Run!”

The White Cock spoke at almost the same time. “Er-ru-u-u-u-u! Run! Run!”

Then all the Hens and Pullets put down their heads and ran as fast as they could for the poultry-house, which was near. The Shanghai Cock and the White Cock waited to let them pass, and then followed in after them. It is a law among fowls that the Cocks must protect the Hens from all danger.

A LARGE DARK BIRD SWOOPING DOWN.

Because these two had to wait so long for the Hens and Pullets to get inside, they were still where they could see quite plainly when the bird, a large Eagle, swooped down to the roof of the carriage-house and caught the Young Cock up in his talons. The Young Cock had not seen him coming until he was almost there. He had been too much interested in watching the fowls on the ground below. When he saw the Eagle it was too late to get away.

As the Eagle flew upward once more, all the fowls ran out to watch him. They could see the Young Cock struggling as the sharp talons of the Eagle held him tightly. "Poor fellow!" said the Pullets. The Cocks were wise enough to keep still. The Hens murmured something to themselves which nobody else could understand. Only the Plymouth Rock Hen said very much about it, and that was because she had children to bring up. One of the Young Cock's tail-feathers floated down from the sky and fell into their yard. "Leave it right there," she said. "Leave it there, and every time you look at it, I want you to remember that the Cock to whom it belonged might now be having a pleasant time on this farm, if he had not been quarrelsome and bragged."

THE GUINEA-FOWLS COME AND GO

It was only a few days after the Young Cock had been carried away by the Eagle, that the Man drove back from town with a very queer look upon his face. A small crate in the back end of the light wagon contained three odd-looking fowls. The Little Girls left their mud pies and ran toward the wagon. When they saw the crate, they ran into the house and called their mother to come out also.

"What have you now?" said she, as she stepped onto the side porch.

"Guinea-fowls," answered the Man. "Just listen to this letter." He drew it from his pocket and read aloud: "I send you, by express, a Guinea-Cock and two Guinea-Hens. They were given to me, and I have no place for keeping them. I remember hearing that they are excellent for scaring away Crows, so I send them on in the hope that they may be useful to you. If you do not wish to keep them, do what you choose with them."

As he read three small and perfectly bald heads were thrust through the openings of the crate and turned and twisted until their owners had seen everything around. "I don't know anything about Guinea-fowls," said the Man, "but I will at least keep these long enough to find out. I have seen the Crows fly down and annoy the Hens several times, and it may be that these are just what we need."

He took the crate down and opened it carefully. The three fowls that walked out looked almost exactly alike. All had very smooth and soft coats of black feathers covered with small round white spots. They were shaped quite like Turkeys, but were much smaller, with gray-brown legs, and heads which were not feathered at all. The skin of their faces and necks was red, and they had small wattles at the corners of their mouths. Bristle-like feathers stood out straight around the upper part of their necks, and below these were soft gray feathers which covered the neck and part of the chest. They walked directly toward the barnyard, where some of the farm fowls were picking up an early dinner. "Ca-mac!" said they "Ca-mac! Ca-mac! We want some too."

Now the farm fowls were not especially polite, not having come of fine families or been taught good manners when they were Chickens, yet they did not at all like to have newcomers speak to them in this way. They noticed it all the more, because when the White Plymouth Rocks came they had acted so very differently. They stepped a little to one side, giving the Guinea-fowls enough room in which to scratch and pick around as they had been doing, but they did not say much to them.

The Gobbler was strutting back and forth among the smaller fowls. He disliked living with them as much as he had to now, but the Hen Turkeys would have nothing to say to him because he annoyed their Chicks. They went off with their children and left him alone, and, as he wanted company of some sort, he took what he could get. He thought it might be a good plan to make friends with the Guinea-fowls.

"Good-morning," said he. "Have you come here to stay?"

"We shall stay if we like it," answered the Guinea-Cock. "We always do what we like best."

"Humph!" said the Shanghai Cock to himself. "Remarkable fowls! Wonder what the Man will think about that."

"I hope you will like it," said the Gobbler, who was so lonely that he really tried hard to be agreeable. "I understand quite how you feel about doing as you like. I always prefer to do what I prefer."

"We *do* it," remarked one of the Guinea-Hens, as she chased the Brown Hen away from the spot where she had been feeding, and swallowed a fat Worm which the Brown Hen had just uncovered.

"Yes," said the other Guinea-Hen, "I guess we are just as good as anybody else."

"Is there plenty to eat here?" asked the Guinea-Cock.

"Plenty," answered the Gobbler. "It is much better than it used to be. There is a new Man here, and he takes better care of his fowls than the Farmer did. He doesn't carry red handkerchiefs either."

"I don't care what kind of handkerchiefs he carries," said the Guinea-Cock. "What makes you talk about such things?"

"You would know what makes me speak of them if you were a Gobbler," was the answer. "I cannot bear red things. I cannot even eat my corn comfortably when anything red is around. You see it is quite important. Anything which spoils a fellow's fun in eating is important."

"Nothing would spoil my fun if I had the right sort of food," remarked the Guinea-Cock. Then he turned to the Guinea-Hens. "Come," he said. "We have eaten enough. Let us walk around and see the place."

All three started off, walking along where-ever they chose, and stopping to feed or to talk about what they saw. Anybody could tell by looking at them that they were related to the Turkeys, but the Gobbler had not cared to remind them of that. He was looking for more company during the time when his own family left him so much alone. He knew that before very long the Turkey Chicks would be too large to fear him, and that when that time came, their mothers and they would be willing to walk with him. Then he would have less to do with the other poultry, and might not want three bad-mannered Guinea-fowl cousins tagging along after him.

Whenever the three met another fowl, they talked about him and said exactly what they thought, and if they passed a Hen who had just found a choice bit of food, they chased her away and ate it themselves. Sometimes they even chased fowls who were not in their way and who were not eating things that they wanted. It seemed as though they had simply made up their minds to do what they wanted to do, whenever and wherever they wished. They did not make much fuss about it, and if you had seen them when they were doing none of these mean things, you would have thought them very genteel. You would never have suspected that they could act as they did.

The Gander and the Geese passed near the Guinea-fowls and the Guinea-fowls did not chase them. They were not foolish enough to annoy people so much larger than they. It is true that the Hens were larger than they, yet the Guinea-fowls could make them run every time. If they had troubled the Geese, it might have ended with the Guinea-fowls doing the running. And the Guinea-fowls were cowards. They would never quarrel with people unless they were sure of beating.

"S-s-s-s-s-s-s!" said the Gander. "Are we to have that sort of people on this farm? If we are, I would rather live somewhere else. I do not see why there should be any disagreeable people anyway."

"There should not be," said the Geese, who always agreed with everything the Gander said, and who really believed as he did about this. "Disagreeable people should be sent away, or eaten up, or something."

Both the Gander and the Geese thought themselves exceedingly agreeable, and so they were—when everything suited them. At other times they were often quite cross. Many people act like this, and seem to think it very sweet of them not to be cross all the time. Truly agreeable people, as you very well know, are those who can keep pleasant when things go wrong.

"Ca-mac!" said the three Guinea-fowls together. "There are some of those stupid Geese, who are always walking around and eating grass that is too short for anybody else. They eat grass, and grow feathers for Farmers' Wives to pluck off. When we have gone to the trouble of growing a fine coat of feathers, we keep them as long as we wish, and then they drop out, a few at a time. If anybody wants our feathers, he must follow around after us and pick them up."

Before night came, the Guinea-fowls had met and annoyed nearly all the poultry on the place. They had even made dashes at the smallest Chickens and frightened them dreadfully. The Man had been too busy to see much of the trouble that they made, but his Little Girls noticed it, for they had been watching the Guinea-fowls and hoping to find some of their beautiful spotted feathers lying around. When the Little Girls were eating their supper of bread and milk, they told their father about it.

"They walk around and look too good for anything," said the brown-haired one, "but whenever they get a chance they chase the Hens and the Chickens."

"Yes," said the golden-haired Little Girl, "I even saw one of them scare the Barred Plymouth Rock Hen, the one who ate bread and salt with you."

"That is very bad," said the Man, gravely. "Any fowl that troubles the Barred Plymouth Rock Hen must be punished."

"What will you do to them?" asked the golden-haired Little Girl. "I think you will have to shut them up. You couldn't spank them, could you? Not even if you wanted to ever so much."

"I shall decide to-night how to punish them," said the Man, "and then in the morning we will see about it." When he spoke he did not know how much time he would spend in thinking about the Guinea-fowls that night.

When it was time for them to go to roost, the Guinea-fowls fluttered and hopped upward until they reached quite a high branch in the apple-tree by the Man's chamber window. Then, instead of going to sleep for the night, as one would think they would wish to do, they took short naps and awakened from time to time to visit with each other. It is true that they had seen much that was new during the day, and so had more than usual to talk about, but this was really no excuse, because they had the habit of talking much at night and would have been nearly as noisy if nothing at all had happened.

The Man was just going to sleep when they awakened from one of their naps and began to chat. "Ca-mac! Ca-mac!" said one. "I suppose those stupid fowls in the poultry-house are sound asleep, with their heads tucked under their wings. What do you think of the company here?"

"Good enough," said another. "I don't like any of them very much, but you can't expect Geese and Ducks to be Guinea-fowls. We don't have to talk to them. The Gobbler is trying to be agreeable, and when the Hen Turkeys can think of any thing besides their children we may find them good company."

"It is a good thing that there are so many Hens here," said the third. "The Man throws out their grain and then we can scare them away and eat all we want of it. What fun it is to see Hens run when they are frightened!"

After this short visit they went to sleep again, and so did the Man. But they went to sleep much more quickly than he did, and he was very tired and disliked being disturbed in that way. He had just fallen asleep when one of the Guinea-Hens awakened again. "Ca-mac!" said she to the others. "Ca-mac! Ca-mac! I have thought of something to say. How do you like the idea of living on this place?"

"We like it," answered the Guinea-Cock and the other Guinea-Hen. Then they went on to tell why they liked it. They said that there were no children of the stone-throwing kind, no Dog, and no Cat. They had plenty of room for the long walks which they liked to take, and there were many chances to get the food which the Man threw out. When they had spoken of all these things the Guinea-Cock said: "It is decided then that we will stay here instead of running away to another farm. This is a good enough place for any fowl. Now let us take another nap."

While they were thinking this, the Man was thinking something quite different. In the morning while the Guinea-fowls were eating grain which had been strewn in one of the yards, the Man closed the gate, and, helped by the Little Girls, drove the three Guinea-fowls into a corner and caught them. Then he put them into the crate in which they had come, and took them across the road to the Farmer who lived there.

When this was done there were many happy people left behind on the poultry-farm. The Little Girls were happy, because they had found four feathers which the Guinea-fowls lost in trying to get away from the Man. The Hens were happy, because they could now be more sure of eating the food which they found. The other poultry were glad to think that they would not have to listen to new-comers saying such dreadful things about them, and perhaps the Man, when he came back, was the happiest of all. "I gave them to the Farmer over there," he said, "and he will give them to a poor family far away. I have stopped keeping Guinea-fowls to scare away the Crows. I would rather keep Crows to scare away the Guinea-fowls, but I think we can get along very comfortably without either." And the poultry thought so too.

THE GEESE AND THE BABY

THE Little Girls had gone to play with a new friend who lived down the road, and the Man was working in the farthest field of the farm. The Baby had been laid in the crib for his afternoon nap, and his mother went up-stairs to work at her house-cleaning. She thought that she might possibly finish two closets if the baby did not awaken and call her too soon. She felt sure that she would know when he awakened, because she left the staircase door ajar, and he usually cried a little as soon as he got his eyes open.

This time, however, the Baby slept only a few minutes and did not cry at all. He had grown a great deal since he came to live on the farm, and was becoming very strong and independent. When he opened his eyes he made no sound, but lay there quietly staring at the ceiling until he heard one of the Cocks crowing outside. He had always wanted to catch that tallest Cock and hug him—he looked so soft and warm—and now was the time to try it. When his mother was around she sometimes held his dress or one of the shoulder-straps of his little overalls and would not let him catch the Cock. He would crawl out of his crib alone and go out very quietly to try it.

The Baby pulled himself up by the rounds of his crib, and tumbled over its railing onto his mother's bed, which stood beside it. From that he slid to the floor. It took him only two minutes more to get out of the side door and down the steps. It did not take at all long for the steps, because he fell more than half the distance. If he had not been running away, or if there had been anybody around to pity him, he would have cried, but to cry now might spoil all his fun, so he picked himself up without making a sound and started for the Shanghai Cock.

The Shanghai Cock was on the ground when the Baby began toddling toward him. As the Baby came nearer he began to walk off. "I don't want to be caught," said he. "It is bad enough to have grown people catch me, but it would be worse to have a Baby do so, for he might choke me."

"Here, pitty Chickie!" said the Baby. "Baby want oo." Then he tried to run, and fell down instead.

The Barred Plymouth Rock Hen looked at him pityingly. "Just the way my Chickens used to act when trying to catch a Grasshopper," said she. "It is so hard for children to learn that they cannot have everything they want."

When the Baby tumbled, the Shanghai Cock stood still, and even picked up a couple of mouthfuls of food. When the Baby got up again, the Shanghai Cock moved on. At last the Cock decided to put a stop to this sort of game, in which the Baby seemed to be having all the fun, so he flew to the top of the pasture fence and crowed as loudly as he could. The Baby's mother heard him as she worked busily upstairs. "How loudly that Cock does crow!" said she. "I am glad that such noises do not wake the Baby. He is having a fine nap to-day." Then she unrolled another bundle of pieces and paid no more attention to the crowing.

When the Baby saw that he could not reach the Cock, he thought he would try for some of the other fowls. The Gobbler came in sight just then and he started after him. Luckily he had no red on, or it might have been the Gobbler who did the chasing. "Here, pitty Chickie!" said the Baby. "Tum, pitty Chickie! Tum to Baby."

It was the first time the Gobbler had ever been been called a "pitty Chickie," but that made no difference. He did not want to be petted and he did not want to be caught. Baby might open and shut his tiny fat hands as many times as he pleased, beckoning to him. The Gobbler would not come. "Gobble-gobble-gobble!" said he. "Nobody can catch me in daylight, not even with corn; and surely nobody can catch me without it." Then he strutted slowly away.

The Baby followed, but when the Gobbler pretended to lose his temper, stood all his feathers on end, spread his fine tail, dragged his wings on the ground, and puffed, the Baby turned and ran away as fast as he could. Brown Bess was no longer in the pasture, and the gate stood open. It was through this gate that the Baby ran, not stopping until he came within sight of the river along the lower edge of the pasture. The water looked so bright and beautiful that he thought he would go farther still. Perhaps he could even catch some of the Ducks and Geese that were swimming there. He had seen his sisters wade in the edge of the river one day, while his father was mending a fence near by. He would wade, too.

You see Baby was only two years old, and did not understand that rivers are very dangerous places for children to visit alone, and worst of all for Babies who toddle and tumble along. He did not know that if he should tumble in that beautiful shining water he might never be able to get up again, or that if he should chase one of the Ducks too far out, he could not turn around and come back to the shore. These things he was not old enough to know. He did know that when he came into the pasture with his father or mother and went toward the river's edge, he was always told, "No-no!" This he remembered, but that made it seem all the more fun to go there when there was nobody by to say it.

The Baby stood on a little knoll near the water. "Here, pitty Chickie!" he said. "Tum to Baby, pitty Chickie!"

The Ducks paid no attention to him, unless it were to swim farther from shore and keep their heads turned slightly toward him, watching to see what he was about. With the Geese, however, it was different.

Geese do not like anything strange, and if they cannot understand a thing they think that there is certainly something wrong. As there is much which they do not understand, the Geese are often greatly excited over very simple and harmless things, hissing loudly at those who are strangers to them. Now they could not understand why the Baby should stand on the river-bank and talk to them. "S-s-s-s-s!" said the Gander. "There must be something wrong about this. Let us get out of the water to see."

He scrambled up onto the bank, with his wife and the other Geese following closely behind him. He was a very stately fellow, and looked as though he could win in almost any fight. The Geese were stately too, but their legs and neck did not look so strong as his, and they let him go ahead and speak first. The Gander marched toward the Baby and stood between him and the river. "S-s-s-s-s!" said he. "What are you doing here?"

"Here, pitty Chickie!" said the Baby. "Tum to Baby."

"I cannot understand you," said the Gander, severely. "Children should speak so that they can be understood. I can always understand my own children." He was very proud of the brood of Goslings which he and his wife had hatched. Perhaps he was even more fond of them because he had done almost as much for them as she, sitting on the eggs part of the time and standing beside her while she was sitting on them. Ganders are excellent fathers.

"Go way, pitty Chickie!" said the Baby. "Baby goin' in de watty."

"S-s-s-s-s!" said the Gander, and this time his wife hissed also. "Go back to the place where you belong. This place is for web-footed people. I have seen your feet uncovered, and you have no webs whatever between your toes. You do not belong here. Go away!"

The Baby did not go away, for he was having a lovely time. The Gander did not come any nearer to him or act as though he meant to peck him, so he just laughed and waved his hands. "Why don't you go?" asked the Geese. "The Gander told you to go away, and you should mind the Gander. We always mind him, and so should you."

Still the Gander and the Geese did not come nearer to him, and still the Baby was not afraid. "S-s-s-s-s!" repeated the Gander. "We do not want you to swim in our river. Your body is not the right shape for swimming with Geese and

Ducks. Your neck is not long enough for feeding in the river. You could never get your mouth down to the river-bottom for food without going way under. Go away! You will get wet if you go into the water. I feel quite sure that you will, for you have not nicely oiled feathers like ours. You will try to catch our children and will make us much trouble. Go away!"

Just then the Baby's mother called from the door of the house. She had come downstairs and found the Baby gone. "Baby!" said she. "Baby! Where are you?"

Baby did not answer, but he turned to look at her. "S-s-s-s-s!" said the Gander and the Geese together. "S-s-s-s-s! S-s-s-s-s!" Then they walked straight for him, and the Baby started home at last. His mother heard and ran toward him in time to see it all. She understood, too, that if it had not been for the Gander and the Geese, her Baby would have gone into the river. That was why she looked so gratefully at them when she reached him and picked him up in her arms to hug and kiss.

Perhaps it was because she had been so frightened that she had to sit right down on a little hillock and rest. The Gander and the Geese stood around and wondered why she made such a fuss over the Baby. "He is nothing remarkable," they said to each other. "He certainly could not swim if he had a chance, and we saw how often he fell down when he tried to run. Why does she put her mouth up against his in that way? There is simply no understanding the actions of people who live in houses."

There was one sort of action which they could understand very well indeed. The Little Girls came home just then and

"S-S-S-S-S!" REPEATED THE GANDER.

their mother had them bring oats from the barn to scatter on the river. Then the Gander, with his wife and the other Geese, gladly went back to the river to feed, for there is nothing which pleases Geese better than to eat oats that are floating on the water.

THE FOWLS HAVE A JOKE PLAYED ON THEM

When the Man first bought the farm and came to live there, he could not understand a thing that his poultry said. This made it very hard for him, and was something which he could not learn from his books and papers. You remember how the Little Girls understood, better than he, what the Cocks meant by crowing so joyfully one day. It is often true that children who think much about such things and listen carefully come to know what fowls mean when they talk.

The Man was really a very clever one, much more clever than the Farmer who had lived there before him, and he decided that since he was to spend much of his time among poultry, he would learn to understand what they were saying. He began to listen very carefully and to notice what they did when they made certain sounds. It is quite surprising how much people can learn by using their eyes and ears carefully, and without asking questions, too.

That was why, before the summer was over, the Man could tell quite correctly, whenever a fowl spoke, whether he was hungry or happy or angry or scared. Not only these, but many other things he could tell by carefully listening. He could not understand a Hen in exactly the way in which her Chickens understand her, but he understood well enough to help him very much in his work. Then he tried talking the poultry language. That was much harder, yet he kept on trying, for he was not the sort of Man to give up just because the task was hard. He had been a teacher for many years, and he knew how much can be done by studying hard and sticking to it.

The Man was very full of fun, too, since he had grown so strong and fat on the farm. He dearly loved a joke, and was getting ready to play a very big joke on some of his poultry.

Anybody who has ever kept Hens knows how hard it is to drive them into the poultry-house when they do not wish to go. People often run until they are quite out of breath and red in the face, trying to make even one Hen go where she should. Sometimes they throw stones, and this is very bad for the Hens, for even if they are not hit, they are frightened, and then the eggs which they lay are not so good. Sometimes, too, the people who are trying to drive Hens lose their temper, and this is one of the very worst things that could happen.

The poultry had not paid much attention to the Man when he was learning their language. They were usually too busy talking to each other to listen to what he was saying. Once the Shanghai Cock said what he thought of it, however: "Just hear him!" he had said. "Hear that Man trying to crow! He does it about as well as a Hen would."

You know a Hen tries to crow once in a while, and then the Cocks all poke fun at her, because she never succeeds well. All this happened before the Man had been long on the farm, and before the Shanghai Cock had learned to like him. The Shanghai Cock would have been very much surprised if anybody had then told him that he would ever be unable to tell the Man's voice from that of one of his best friends.

Throughout the summer the fowls who had always lived on the farm were allowed to run wherever they wished during the day, and were not driven into the pen at night. There was always some corn scattered in their own yard for them just before roosting-time, and they were glad enough to stroll in and get it. When they finished eating they were sure to find the outer gate closed, and then they went inside the pen to roost. Now, however, the days were growing much shorter and the nights cooler, and a Skunk had begun prowling around after dark. The Man decided that if he wanted to keep his poultry safe, he must have them in the pens quite early and shut all the openings through which a night-hunting animal might enter to catch them. He liked to attend to this before he ate his own supper, and the poultry did not wish to go to roost quite so early. They often talked of it as they ate their supper in the yard.

"I think," said the Brown Hen, "that something should be done to stop the Man's driving us into the pen before we are ready to go. It is very annoying."

"Annoying?" said the White Cock, who was a great friend of hers. "I should say it is annoying! I hadn't half eaten my supper last night when I heard him saying, 'Shoo! Shoo!' and saw him and the Little Girls getting ready to drive us in."

"Well, you might better eat a little faster the next time,"

said the Black Hen. "I saw you fooling around when you might have been eating, and then you grumbled because you hadn't time to finish your supper."

"I would rather fool around a little than to choke on a big mouthful, the way you did," replied the White Cock, who did not often begin a quarrel, but was always ready to keep it up. "I was hungry all night," he added.

"It is so senseless," said the Brown Hen. "He might just as well drive us in after we have had time enough for our supper, or even wait until we go in without driving. I have made up my mind not to go to-night until I am ready."

"What if they try to drive you?" asked the White Cock.

"I will run this way and that, and flutter and squawk as hard as I can," replied the Brown Hen.

The Black Hen laughed in her cackling way. "I will do the same," said she. "It will serve the Man right for trying to send us to roost so early. I think he will find it pretty hard work."

The White Cock would make no promises. He wanted to see the Hens run away from the Man, but thought he would rather stand quietly in a corner than to flutter around. He was afraid of acting like a Hen if he made too much fuss, and no Cock wishes to act like a Hen.

The Shanghai Cock felt in the same way. "I am too big for running to and fro," said he, "but I will keep out of the pen and watch the fun."

He had hardly spoken these words when the Man and the Little Girls came into the yard and closed the gate behind them. The poultry kept on eating, but watched them as they ate. Suddenly the Brown Hen picked up a small boiled potato that she had found among the other food, and ran with it in her bill to the farthest corner of the yard. The Black Hen ran after her and the other Hens after them. The Cocks remained behind and watched.

The Man and the Little Girls tried to get between the Hens and the farthest side of the fence. The Hens would not let them for a while, but kept running back and forth there, until the potato had fallen to pieces and been trampled on without any one having a taste. When the Man and the Little Girls finally got behind the Hens, the Little Girls spread out their skirts and flapped them and the Man said, "Shoo! Shoo!"

Then the Hens acted dreadfully frightened, and the Cocks began to turn their heads quickly from side to side, quite as though they were looking for a chance to get away. They were really having a great deal of fun. Whenever the Man thought that he had them all ready to go into the open door of the pen, one of the Hens would turn with a frightened squawk and flutter wildly past him again to the back end of the yard, and then the Man would have to begin all over. Several of the Hens dropped loose feathers, and it was very exciting.

"Well," said the Shanghai Cock, as the Man went back the fifth time for a new start, "I think that Man will leave us alone after to-night."

"Yes," said the White Cock, who was standing near him, "I think we are teaching him a lesson."

He spoke quite as though he and the other Cock were doing it, instead of just standing by and watching the Hens. But that is often the way with Cocks.

After the Man had tried once more and failed, he certainly acted as though he was ready to give up the task. He walked to the back end of the yard, took off his hat, and wiped his forehead with his handkerchief. The Little Girls stood beside him, and he picked up a feather to show them. It was a wing-feather, and he was showing them how the tiny hooks on each soft barb caught into those on the next and held it firmly.

The poultry watched him for a while and then began eating once more. They thought him quite discouraged.

The Shanghai Cock and the White Cock were standing far apart when somebody called "Er-ru-u-u-u-u!" which is the danger signal. As soon as he heard it, each Cock thought that the other had spoken, and opened his bill and said, "Er-ru-u-u-u-u!" in the same tone, even before he looked around for a Hawk or an Eagle.

Every Hen in the yard ducked her head and ran for the door of the pen as fast as her legs would carry her. The Cocks let the Hens go ahead and crowd through the doorway as well as they could, but they followed closely behind. They were hardly inside when the door of the pen was closed after them and they heard the Man fastening it on the outside.

"Wasn't that a shame!" said the Brown Hen, who always thought that something was a shame. "We didn't finish our supper after all!"

"I know it," said the White Cock. "It happened very badly, and all that running had made me hungry."

"What was the danger?" asked the Shanghai Cock. "I had no time to see whether it was an Eagle or a Hawk coming."

"What do you mean?" cried the White Cock. "If I had

given the alarm which took all my friends from their supper into the pen, I think I would take time to see what the danger was. Can't you tell one kind of bird from another?"

"I can if I see them," answered the Shanghai Cock, rather angrily. "I did not see this one. I looked up as soon as you gave the cry, but I saw nothing. I repeated the cry, as Cocks always do, but I saw nothing."

"Now see here," said the White Cock, as he lowered his head and looked the Shanghai Cock squarely in the eyes, "you stop talking in this way! You gave the first warning and you know it. I only repeated the call."

"I did not," retorted the Shanghai Cock, as he lowered his head and ruffled his feathers. "*You* gave the warning and *I* repeated it."

"He did not," interrupted the Brown Hen. "I stood right beside him, and I know he did not give the first call."

"Well," said the Barred Plymouth Rock Hen, "I was standing close to the Shanghai Cock, and *I* know that *he* did not give the first call." (Her Chickens were now so large that they did not need her, and she had begun running with her old friends.)

Then arose a great chatter and quarrel in the pen. Part of the Hens thought that the White Cock gave the first warning, and part of them thought that the Shanghai Cock did. Everybody was out of patience with somebody else, and all were scolding and finding fault until they really had to stop for breath. It was when they stopped that the Speckled Hen spoke for the first time. She had never been known to quarrel, and she was good-natured now.

"I believe it was the White Plymouth Rock Cock in the other yard," said she. "Why didn't we think of that before?"

"Of course!" said all the fowls together. "It was certainly the White Plymouth Rock Cock in the other yard." Then they laughed and spoke pleasantly to each other as they began to settle themselves for the night. "We might as well go to roost now," they said, "even if it is a bit early. All that running and talking was very tiring."

But it was not the White Plymouth Rock Cock who had said "Er-ru-u-u-u-u!" He and his Hens had run into their pen at the same time, and had been shut in. Only the Man and the Little Girls knew who it really was, and they never told the poultry.

THE LITTLE GIRLS GIVE A PARTY

LATE in the fall, when the Man began to talk of shutting the poultry into their own yards for the winter, there came a few mild and lovely days. The Little Girls had been playing out-of-doors in their jackets, but now they left them in the house and ran around bare-headed, as they had done during the summer. All the poultry were happy over the weather, and several said that, if they thought it would last long enough, they would like to raise late broods of Chickens.

The fowls had finished moulting, and had fine coats of new feathers to keep them warm through the winter. The young Turkeys looked more and more like their mothers, for they were already nearly as large as they ever would be. The Goslings and the Ducklings had grown finely, and boasted that their legs and feet began to look rougher and more like those of the old Geese and Ducks. The Chickens were all White Plymouth Rocks this year, and the tiny red combs which showed against the snowy feathers of their heads made them very pretty. Even the Hens who had cared for them since they were hatched would not have had them any other color, although at first they had wished that their Chickens could look more like them.

In the barn all was neat and well cared for. The Man had made Brownie a warm box-stall, so that he need not be tied in a cool and narrow place whenever he stood in the barn, but might turn around and take a few steps in any direction he chose. There was plenty of fine hay in the loft for him, and the place where Brown Bess and her Calf were to stand had also been made more comfortable. There were great bins filled with grain for the poultry, and another full of fine gravel for them to eat with their meals. They had no teeth and could not chew their food, you know, so they had to swallow enough gravel, or grit, for their stomachs to use in grinding it and getting the strength out. In another place was a great pile of dust for winter dust-baths.

Everything was so well prepared for cold weather that it seemed almost funny to have warm days again. And just at this time the Little Girls had a birthday. Not two birthdays, you understand, but one, for they were twins and were now exactly six years old. They were plump and rosy Little Girls, and very strong from living so much out-of-doors. Each had a new doll for a birthday gift, and the funniest part of it was that the brown-haired Little Girl had a brown-haired doll and the golden-haired Little Girl had a golden-haired doll. That made it easy to tell which doll was which, just as the difference in hair made it easy for their parents to tell one twin from the other.

When they first awakened they were given birthday kisses instead of birthday spanks, six apiece for the years they had lived, a big one on which to grow, and another big one on which to be good. After the breakfast dishes were washed and put away, their mother made two birthday cakes for the Little Girls and put six candles on each. With all this done for them, one would certainly expect the Little Girls to be perfectly happy. But, what do you think? They could not be perfectly, blissfully happy, because they were not to have a party.

Every year before this, as far back as they could remember, they had been allowed to have a party, and this year they could not have it, because they were living on a farm and there were no other children who could come. It is true that there were two others living quite near, but these two had the measles and could not go to parties. By the time they were over the measles, the birthday would be long past, and so the Little Girls were disappointed.

It was when the brown-haired Little Girl was telling her doll about the last year's party, and the golden-haired Little Girl's eyes were filling with tears, that their mother had a bright idea. She would not tell them what it was, but asked them to care for the Baby while she went out to talk with the Man in the barn.

When she came back she told them that they might have a party after all and invite the poultry to come. "I think it will be great fun," said she, "and I am sure they have never been to a birthday party in their lives."

How happy the Little Girls were then! The Man had put a very large box just in front of the poultry-yards where the White Plymouth Rocks were kept, so that, by crowding into the corners, the Chickens on one side of the separating fence and the Cock and Hens on the other could come quite near to the box. Inside the big box was another which was to be their table, and a couple of milking stools on which they were to sit. The Baby's chair was to be brought when he came.

Of course it seemed a long time to wait until afternoon, when the party was to come off. If there had not been so much to do, the Little Girls certainly could not have been patient. It was wonderful how many things their mother could suggest. In the first place, they had to write a few invitations to pin up where the fowls could see them. Then they had to go over to the edge of the woods and hunt all along the roadside to find late flowers, bits of brake, and autumn leaves, with which to trim their box and the table. After that they took pans and got grain for their guests from the bins in the barn. These they carried to the big box and placed on the table inside. It was not long afterward that the brown-haired Little Girl found the Black Hen and the White Cock eating from these pans. "Oh, shoo!" she cried, running as fast as she could toward them and flapping her skirts. "Shoo! Shoo! It isn't time for you to come, and you mustn't eat up the party yet."

The other twin feared that, after being frightened away in this fashion, these two fowls would not want to come at the proper time, but she need not have worried. Fowls are always glad to come to a good supper, and there is much more danger of their coming too early and staying too late than there is of their not coming at all. After that the pans of grain were carried into the house to wait until the right time.

In the afternoon the twins and their dolls came out to

the big box which they pretended was their house. The open side of it was toward the poultry-yards, and there was plenty of room between for the fowls who were running free to come in and get their food. The Little Girls had wanted to put on their Sunday dresses, but their mother told them that she did not think it would be really polite to the poultry, who had to wear the very same feathers that they had on every day. So the Little Girls contented themselves with having their hair done up on top of their heads and bows of yellow tissue paper pinned on the knots. This made them feel very fine indeed, and as though being six years old were almost the same as being grown up. They had some beautiful red tissue paper which they wanted to use, but when they remembered how the Gobbler felt about red, they decided to use the yellow instead. And that was both wise and kind. One should always try to make guests happy.

The Baby was not to come out until supper-time, so the Little Girls and their dolls played quite alone for a while. There was much to tell and to show the dolls, for it was the first time they had ever been on a farm, and everything must have seemed strange to them.

"Do you see that tall White Plymouth Rock Cock over there?" said the brown-haired twin to hers. "My Father says he is the most vallyoobol fowl on the farm. He cost a lot of money. I asked Father if he paid as much as ten cents for him, and he said he paid a great deal more. Just think of that! More than ten cents! You must be very polite to him."

"I will show you our kindest Hen," said the golden-haired twin to her doll. "She is coming this way now. She is the Barred Plymouth Rock Hen, and she is a peticullar friend of my Father's. She didn't cost so much as some of the others, but she is very good."

"And there comes the Speckled Hen," said the brown-haired twin. "She doesn't lay many eggs, but my Father says that she is the best Hen on the farm about taking care of lonely or sick Chickens. She is very small, but she spreads herself out so she can cover a lot, and then she cuddles them until they are happy again, and can run around with her and eat the Worms she scratches up for them."

There is no telling how much more the dolls might have learned about their new neighbors, if the Baby and the mother of the Little Girls had not come out just then. The Baby was put in his chair in the big box and given a cracker to eat, while the Little Girls stood outside and called to their company.

"Come, Chick, Chick, Chick!" they called. "Come, Chick, Chick, Chick!"

From far and near the Hens came running, with lowered heads and hurrying feet, to seize the food which they knew would be given them after that call. The Shanghai Cock and the White Cock followed more slowly, as was their habit. The Gander waddled gravely along from the farthest corner of the pasture in which the poultry-house stood, with his wife and the other Geese following solemnly behind him. The Turkeys, all together once more since the children were so large, came with rather more haste from the roadside, where they had been hunting acorns. And down by the river the Ducks and their children could be seen scrambling up onto the bank and shaking themselves. All were glad enough to come to the party as soon as they were sure it was time, but whether they had understood the invitations which had been pinned around for them to read—well, who can tell about that?

The Man came from the barn to see the fun, and he and the Woman set the two birthday cakes from her basket onto the table. After she had done that, she had to pay more attention to the Baby, who kept trying to reach them with his fat little hands. The Man handed a pan of corn to each of the Little Girls. "Wait until the Ducks get here," he said. "They must have their share and there is plenty of time."

The brown-haired Little Girl felt that those who were waiting should be amused in some way, so she began to talk to them. "This is our birthday party," she said, "and we are very glad you didn't have the measles, so you could come. A party is something to eat when you are dressed up and have company. We have some corn for you because you like that best, but if you are good and polite you may have some of our cake, too."

By this time the Ducks were there, and each Little Girl began flinging handfuls of corn out to the poultry. Some of it was thrown into the yards where the White Plymouth Rocks were kept, and the rest fell between the yards and the big box. One cannot say very much for the manners of the company, yet it is quite certain that they had a good time. When they had settled down to eating quietly, the Man lighted the candles on the birthday cakes and the Woman passed a plate of bread and butter sandwiches to the three happy children around the table. The dolls did not seem to be hungry, but they must have enjoyed it very much, for they smiled all the time, even when nobody was speaking to them.

The Man and the Woman sat on a couple of old Chicken-coops by the open side of the big box, and said what a fine day it was, and how good everything tasted, and what a very large party it was. The Baby laughed a great deal and said "Pitty! Pitty!" every time a soft breeze made the candle-flames dip and waver. The most exciting time came when the candles burned low and had to be blown out by the Little Girls, with the Baby helping.

Then the cakes were cut, and the Man and the Woman and the three children in the box all had a share. The dolls were not forgotten, but even after they had been fed there was much remaining. The Barred Plymouth Rock Hen stepped daintily up to the box and stood with her left foot lifted.

"My friend, the Hen, is hinting that we should pass the cake to the other guests," said the Man, "and I think we should."

The Little Girls helped to cut it into small pieces, and then the whole family, Baby, and all, stood in the sunshine and threw the fragments to the eager poultry, while the dolls looked on. The Barred Plymouth Rock Hen walked inside the box and picked up the many crumbs around the table, while the other fowls fluttered and ran for the pieces outside. The Black Hen always picked for the largest, and the rest chased her. Their manners were certainly bad, but it was the first birthday party they had ever attended, and perhaps it is not strange that they were excited and greedy.

When the last crumb had been thrown out and not even the Black Hen could find another scrap, the Man and his family turned toward the house. The sun was already low in the sky, and the air grew cooler as night drew near. It reminded the Man that winter was coming. "It has been a happy summer," he said, "a busy and happy summer. I am strong again, and the work has gone well. I have a fine lot of fowls, and I am fond and proud of them. I think they deserve a party once in a while."

"It was the very nicest party we ever had," said the Little Girls. "We ought to invite the poultry every time."

The Barred Plymouth Rock Hen murmured softly as she walked along behind them.

"She thinks so too," said the Man.